D0849836

Bulleid
Locomotives

Previous page: With just three weeks of steam operations left, and showing signs of wear and tear, 'Battle of Britain' Pacific No 34057 *Biggin Hill* stands in Nine Elms shed. The front numberplate and the nameplates had been removed, but some-one had been busy with white paint on the front end. The BR AWS battery box is well illustrated, mounted above the bufferbeam./*Ian G. Holt*

Below: The airsmoothed outer casing of the Bulleid Pacifics enabled the SR publicity department to produce larger than normal named trained headboards and decorations. 'Battle of Britain' Pacific No 34071 *601 Squadron* heads the 'Thanet Belle' Pullman near Rainham on 20 September 1950. The engine is in a mixed livery of Malachite green, but with BR emblem and lettering, which was rather an attractive combination. Note the hole cut in the nameboard for the central lower headlight on the locomotive. / *British Rail SR*

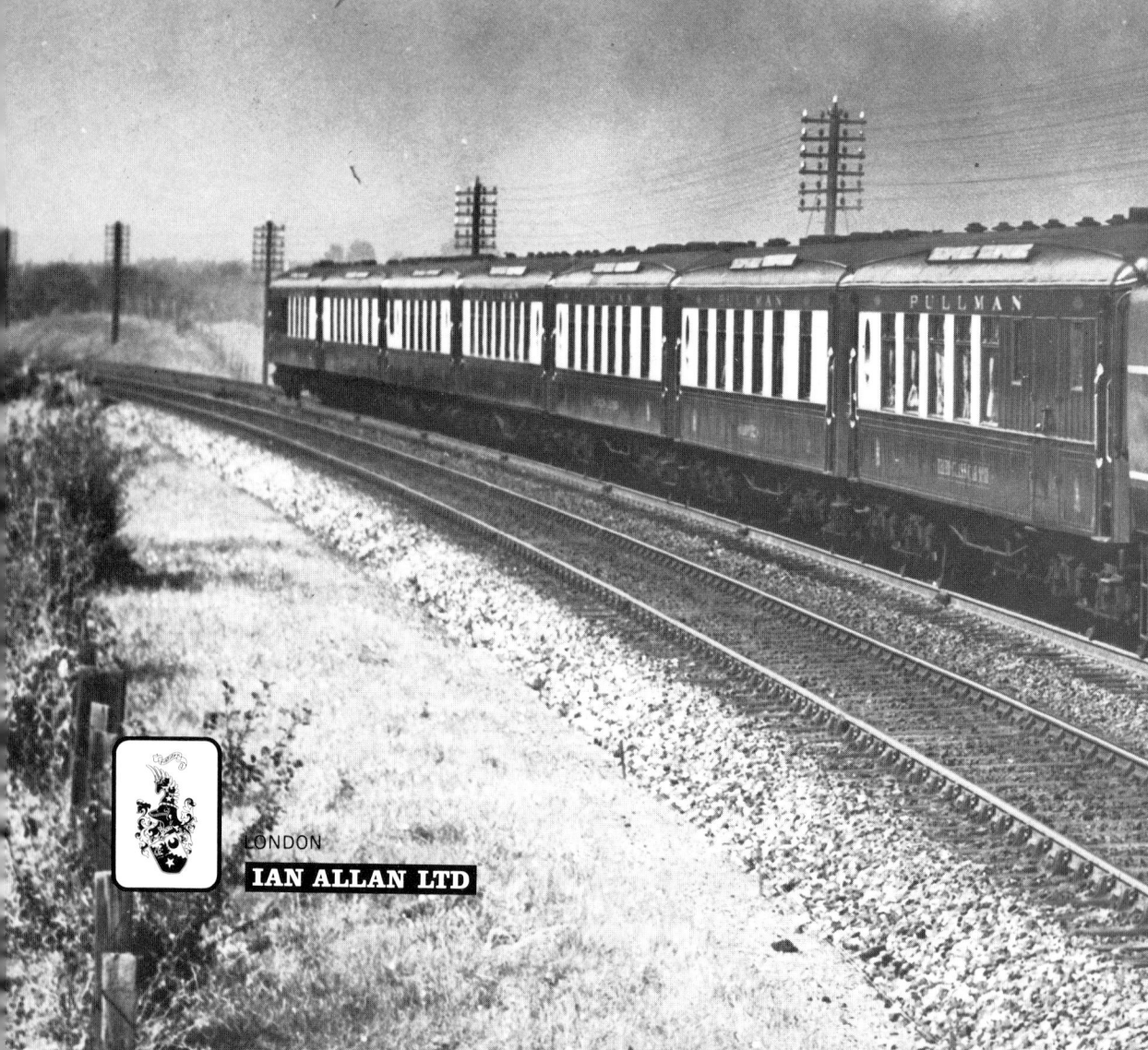

LONDON

IAN ALLAN LTD

Bulleid
Locomotives

A
Pictorial
History by
Brian Haresnape

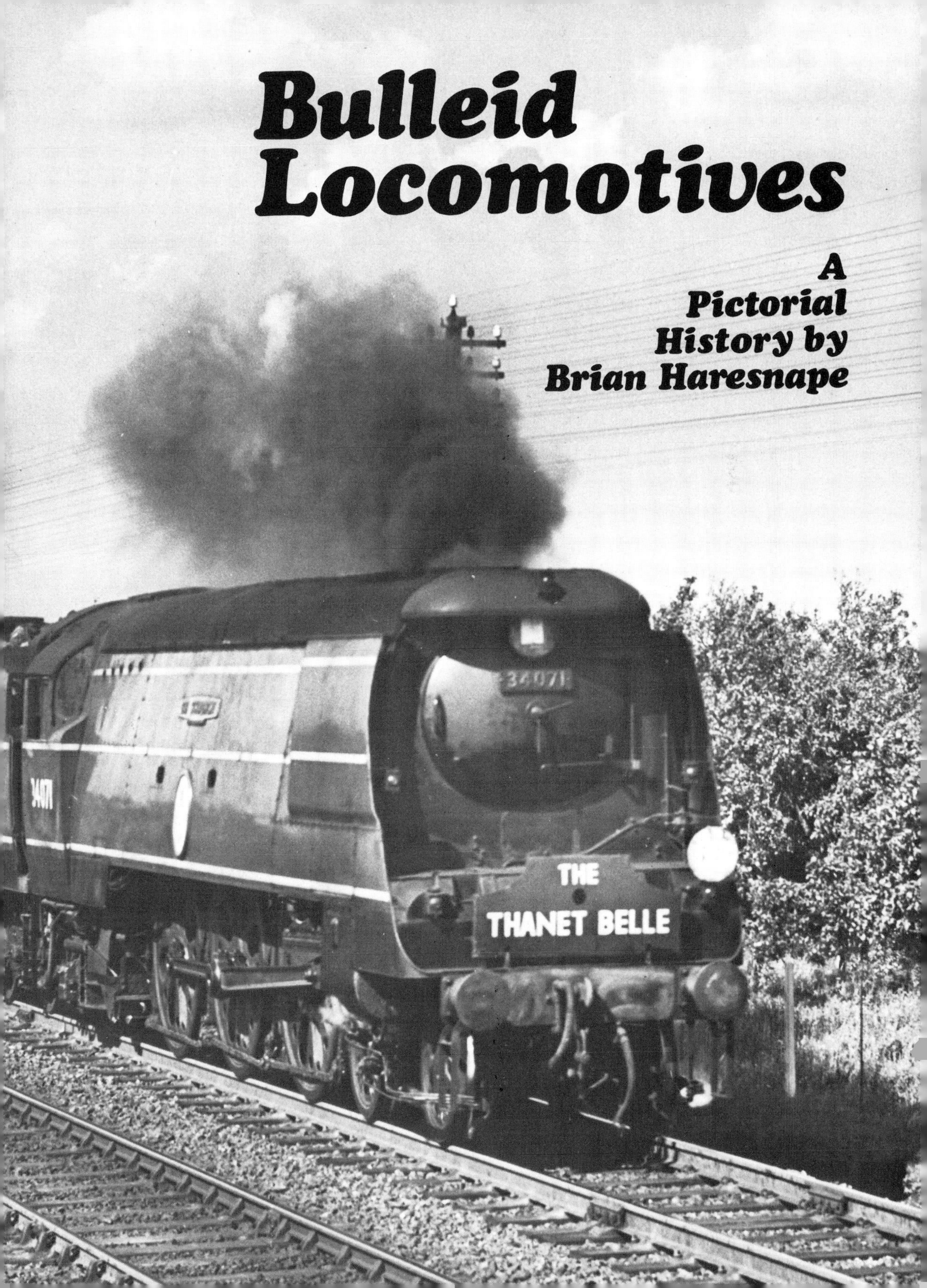

First published 1977
Reprinted 1979

ISBN 0 7110 0794 2

© Brian Haresnape 1977

Published by Ian Allan Ltd, Shepperton, Surrey;
and printed in the United Kingdom by Ian Allan Printing Ltd

For my mother, who encouraged my boyhood enthusiasm for steam locomotives

Below: 'Battle of Britain' class 4-6-2 No 34074 *46 Squadron* at Stewarts Lane Shed./*E. Rixon*

Contents

Author's Note to Second Edition
Since the first edition of this book was published, in 1977, there have been a number of changes in the lists of locomotives preserved, or scheduled for preservation. All references in the text to 'at the time of writing' should therefore be compared to the following up-dated details (correct at time of going to press).

Addenda
Page 55 (last of class withdrawn) delete: reference to 34023. (examples preserved — unrebuilt) add: 34092, 34105.
Page 61 (examples preserved — unrebuilt) add: 34081. Delete existing reference to 34081/92.
Page 85 (examples preserved) delete: 35009 (see below).
Page 97 (examples preserved) add: 34101.
In addition to those actually preserved, the following locomotives were still intact at Barry scrapyard in January 1979, and some may still be rescued for preservation: 34007, 34010, 34027, 34028, 34046, 34053, 34058, 34059, 34067, 34070, 34072, 34073, 35006, 35009, 35010, 35011, 35018, 35022, 35025, 35027.

Foreword

Introduction

All fascinating subjects repay detailed examination and there are many veins of intricate detail in the huge arena of steam locomotives. But often a step back from detail is rewarding, to picture as a whole the locomotives of one type, or one railway, or one designer. Then one gets a grand impression of the general scene, as of the Bulleid engines so admirably presented in this pictorial history.

Though ready to improve the smallest detail, O. V. S. Bulleid was himself very keen on a clear view of the general scene. He liked those pictorial mile-by-mile descriptions of railway routes, and illustrated features as in *Country Life,* and he would have liked to see pictorial histories of anyone's steam locomotives, not least his own.

Steam engines are like the best sculptures of human and animal figures. In them one recognizes brain, body and limbs. By the pose one tells their work or intent. But the steam engine can go into action, leaving the sculpture standing. Here specially a pictorial history scores by presenting these attractive iron horses as they go about their wide-ranging duties.

This pictorial history displays the Bulleid locomotives in all moods, from repose to demonaic energy. It gives a grand parade of a fine stud of engines.

H. A. V. Bulleid.

No one, it seems, was more surprised than Bulleid himself when, in May 1937, he was sent for by Sir Herbert Walker, the Chairman of the Southern Railway, and told that he could have the job of CME of the Southern if he would apply for it. The retiring Chief Mechanical Engineer, R. E. L. Maunsell, stayed on during the September in which Bulleid settled in, and on 1 October 1937 Bulleid took over completely.

Prior to this unexpected change, Bulleid had been Assistant to Nigel Gresley, the CME of the LNER, and had been absorbed in technical and experimental work for many years, being closely involved with all the many Gresley triumphs and achievements. Suddenly he found himself the "Chief" and confronted, with a railway which in recent years had devoted more time, energy and money to electric traction than to steam. The results of Bulleid's transformation of Southern steam power between the immediate pre-World War 2 days and the nationalisation of the railways in 1948 forms the larger part of the contents of this pictorial history.

Born in New Zealand on 19 September 1882 of British parents, O. V. S. Bulleid came to Britain in 1889 upon the death of his father. His childhood and early teens were spent in Accrington living with relatives and he then obtained a four-year premium apprenticeship under H. A. Ivatt at the Doncaster works of the Great Northern Railway, commencing on 21 January, 1901. By January 1907 he had become Assistant to the Locomotive Works Manager. But Bulleid was ambitious and at this point he succeeded in obtaining a job in France; he left the GNR in December, to become the Assistant Works Manager and Chief Draughtsman of the French Westinghouse Company, at their Freinville works near Paris. Next he obtained the post of Mechanical Engineer to the Exhibitions Branch of the Board of Trade, for the Brussels (1910) and Turin (1911) Exhibitions.

In December 1911, with his latest job at an end, Bulleid (by now a married man of 29 with a year-old daughter) returned to Doncaster and sought to rejoin the GNR. He became Personal Assistant to Gresley, who was then taking over

Above: Maunsell 'Lord Nelson' class 4-6-0 No 863 *Lord Rodney* alongside Bulleid 'Battle of Britain' class 4-6-2 No 21C160 (then unnamed) at Waterloo on 20 March 1948. The Maunsell engine has the improved front end, with multiple-jet blastpipe and large diameter chimney, which was one of Bulleid's first design improvements following his appointment as Chief Mechanical Engineer of the Southern Railway. He made similar modifications to other classes of Maunsell locomotive, including a few 'King Arthurs'./*C. C. B. Herbert*

Left: Bulleid-Firth-Brown (BFB) disc centre wheels on a 'Battle of Britain' Pacific; also showing the slide bar cover which was applied to some engines in an attempt to prevent sand from the leading sandpipe reaching the motion. The cylinder cocks, with rodding and the clasp brake gear, are also well illustrated. /*Ian Allan Library*

as Locomotive, Carriage & Wagon Superinten-
dent. Thus began their close association which
spanned more than a quarter of a century, in-
terrupted for Bulleid only by four years of war
service from 1915 to 1919. With the formation
of the London & North Eastern Railway,
Gresley became CME and Bulleid was
appointed as his assistant, with offices in
London, in the early months of 1923. Bulleid's
activities, which ranged widely from carriage
and wagon design to locomotive testing and
technical experiments of many kinds, are
outside the scope of the present volume, which
is only concerned with the locomotives
designed by him after leaving the LNER.
Nevertheless, it is clear that many of his ex-
periences working alongside Gresley were to
colour his attitudes in later years.

In retrospect, Bulleid was a born inventor
and one, moreover, with an insatiable appetite
for trying out his ideas in practice. He loved
visiting outside firms to see their methods and
ideas, and particularly in his later years (when
concerned with the dieselisation of the Irish
National Rail system) he took delight in the
design alternatives that were tendered by
outside contractors. Whilst working with
Gresley he succeeded in getting a number of his

Above: Bulleid was impressed by the performance of the Maunsell
'Schools' class 4-4-0s, but nevertheless included them in his
programme for improved front-end, with multiple-jet blastpipe.
Not all the engines were dealt with, as the improvement was
marginal. No 30924 *Haileybury* is seen with the large-diameter
Bulleid chimney, in hybrid livery of SR Malachite green and early
BR renumbering with 'Southern' on the tender, c. 1948. A similar
modification was applied to some of the Maunsell Q class 0-6-0s
/*A. C. Cawston*

Above right: An impressive angle to view a 'Merchant Navy' as No
35028 leans to the curve through Clapham Junction with the
down 6.30pm Waterloo to Bournemouth express on 27 June
1949. The nameplates are boarded over, pending the official
naming ceremony. The profile of the tender matched the post-war
Bulleid passenger stock./*C. C. B. Herbert*

Right: Memories of summer holidays in the past, with Malachite
green engines in lush West Country landscapes, are evoked by
'West Country' class Pacific No 34019 *Bideford* heading an
Exeter – Plymouth local at Dainton, WR, with a train of ex-LMS
stock, still in maroon livery./*J. G. Hubback*

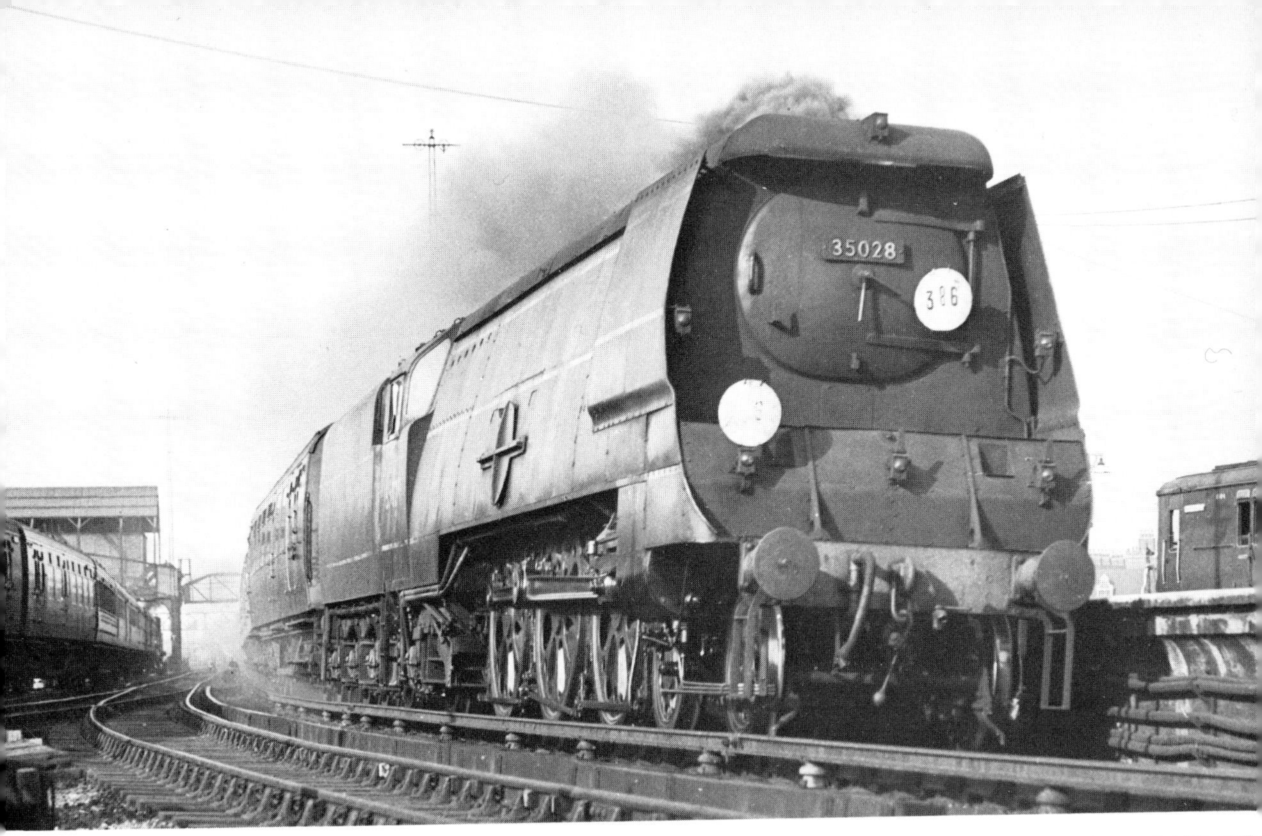
35028
386

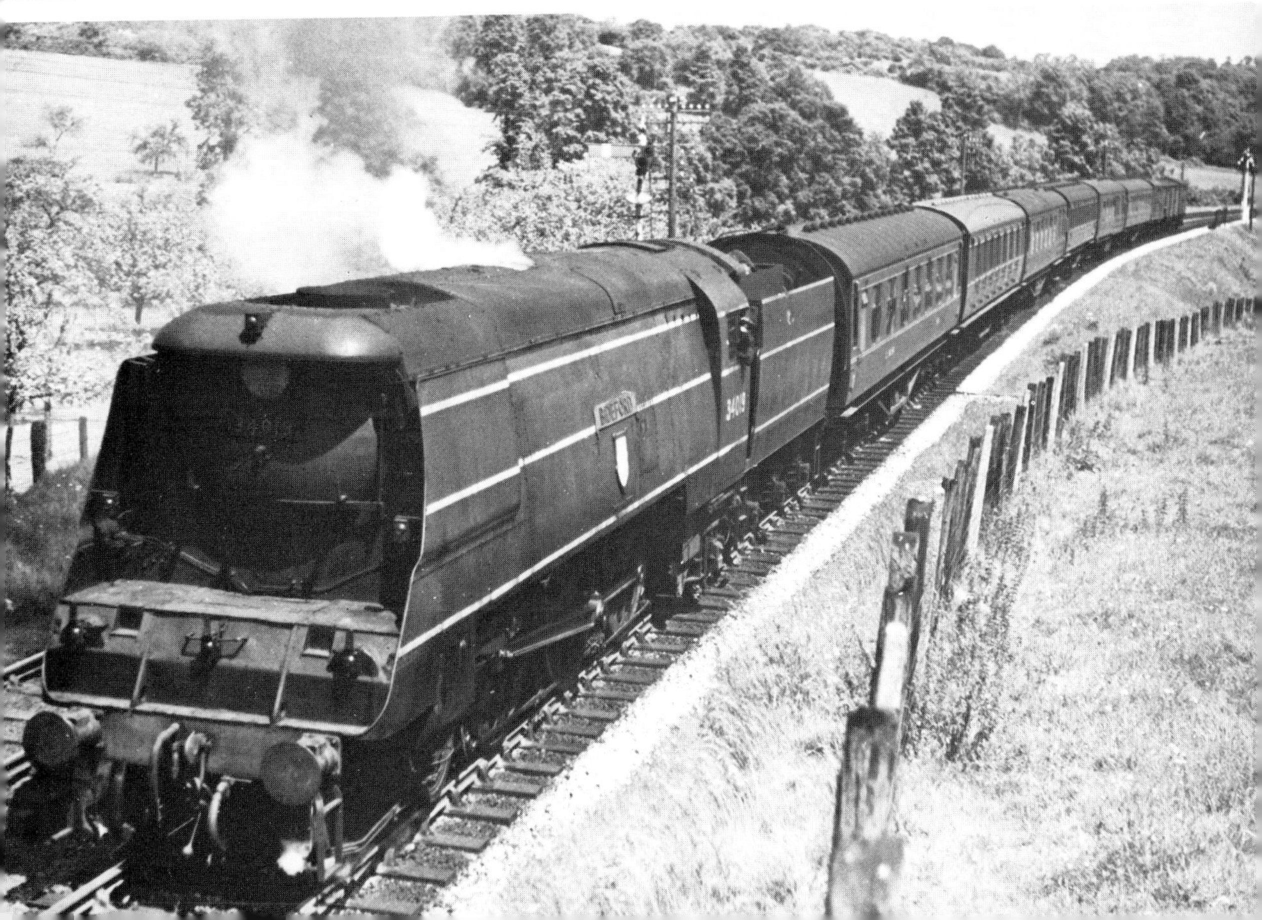

Above: One of the most controversial steam locomotives ever designed, the unique 'Leader' class 0-6-6-0T was Bulleid's last design for the Southern Railway and in fact did not appear until after nationalisation. One of the least satisfactory aspects proved to be the fireman's compartment, which became unbearably hot. The fireman is visible, leaning well out of the cab and with the door part-open in this view of No 36001 on a trial run near Lewes. Oil-firing (as originally intended by Bulleid) would have reduced the problem to some extent./*Author's collection*

Left: The last version of the classic British 0-6-0 goods engine was also the most bizarre in appearance, due to a need to keep down weight. Bulleid was quick to observe that the appearance of his new Q1 class engines was the result of form following function. No 33013 was photographed coaling at Guildford shed./*P. F. Winding*

pet schemes tried out and subsequently adopted, sometimes getting his knuckles rapped by his Chief in the process!

One locomotive of the Gresley era, in particular, seems to have a bearing on what followed on the Southern. This was the magnificent 2–8–2 passenger engine *Cock o' the North,* intended for the heavy trains and difficult grades of the Edinburgh-Aberdeen line. Bulleid and Gresley worked in close accord on the design of this engine and in it one may see the genesis of Bulleid's later Pacifics. In fact, at one stage he considered a 2–8–2 design for the SR duties which the 'Merchant Navy' Pacifics eventually undertook. Externally *Cock o' the North* had unusual lines for a British locomotive, and the front end arrangement with sloping top to the smokebox and integral smoke deflectors carried forward from the boiler casing were features to be seen in modified form on No 21C1 *Channel Packet* in her original condition.

One of Bulleid's first actions on arrival at Waterloo was personally to test the existing main-line motive power, by making footplate runs. An early result was the provision of improved front end and exhaust for the Maunsell 'Lord Nelson' class, also for some of the 'Schools' and a handful of 'King Arthurs'. Unfortunately whilst the multiple-jet Lemaître exhaust used by Bulleid certainly invigorated the locomotives concerned it did nothing for their appearance!

Right: Perhaps the genesis of the Bulleid Pacific front-end may be seen in Gresley's Class P2 2–8–2 No 2001 *Cock o' the North* with the sloping top to the smokebox and the smoke deflectors incorporated into the boiler casing. Bulleid was closely involved in the design and testing of this engine, whilst on the LNER./*British Rail*

Below: Drifting exhaust has momentarily completely obscured the driver's vision as a blustery wind beats against 'Merchant Navy' Pacific No 35014 *Nederland Line,* seen near Basingstoke on 8 September, 1952. This was a constant problem with the air-smoothed casing of the Bulleid engines, partly due to the prevailing south-west winds of the region in which they operated and partly inherent in the front-end design. Many attempts were made to overcome this feature, without any great success./*Roy E. Wilson*

Below right: A handsome transformation. The removal of Bulleid's air-smoothed casing and the application of Walschaerts valve gear when the engines were modified by British Railways (as described in Part Two on pages 78-89) produced a locomotive of impressive appearance, not unlike the larger BR standard designs. No 35023 *Holland-Afrika Line* was photographed at Southampton Central on 2 March 1957. The tender was the last to receive from Eastleigh works the old-style BR lion-and-wheel emblem./*G. Wheeler*

A report on the state of the existing steam stock, plus Bulleid's powers of persuasion, resulted in Southern Railway agreement to a steam locomotive modernisation scheme. First on the list was what was described as a fast mixed-traffic locomotive. This was envisaged as a 4–8–2 capable of good acceleration, a top speed sufficient for 75 mph bookings and good route availability for both passenger and freight workings. Turntable limitations forced the reduction of overall length to a 2–8–2 wheel arrangement, which produced hostile reactions from the Civil Engineer, until a Helmholtz pony truck was proposed; then Bulleid did, in fact, get agreement for two 2–8–2s to be built for trials. He nevertheless foresaw problems in gaining acceptance, and proposed a 4–6–2 alternative, which was more readily agreed upon. The resulting 'Merchant Navy' Pacific is described on pages 18-35.

In retrospect it seems that Bulleid was always the victim of time. He arrived on the Southern just as the winds of war were beginning to unsettle the nation. By the time his first locomotive was ready Britain was in the darkest days of World War 2. His second locomotive design, the ugly Q1 0–6–0, was essentially an engine of war, produced for a specific and urgent need. Towards the end of the war it was possible to plan for peacetime and the Light Pacifics emerged in quantity in the immediate post-war months. But already another change was on the horizon, in the form of the impending nationalisation of the railways, and Bulleid was approaching retirement age as he worked on the design of his highly unconventional 'Leader' class. Even in Ireland, where he went after leaving the Southern, his 'Turf Burner' was produced at the eleventh hour of steam, and was overtaken by a decision to dieselise the entire CIE system.

A very considerable amount has been written both for and against the Bulleid locomotives. There is no doubt that some of the more unconventional features he introduced did not prove satisfactlory in everyday service, and the operating department viewed them with considerable dislike, in particular the chain-driven valve gear of the Pacifics and the oil-bath which encased it. The engines steamed well, in particular the superb boilers on the Pacifics, but they were heavy on coal and oil. They showed a fine turn of speed on many occasions but their day-to-day availability was not high by existing standards. They were unpredictable, and their behaviour ranged from magnificent to downright unpleasant from the enginemen's viewpoint. A recently shopped Pacific would sparkle in its performance, delighting train recorders with their stopwatches, but at high cost.

Personally I have a great affection for them, as I lived near the West of England main line when the Pacifics were in their heyday. The Malachite green livery suited their odd exterior very well and they looked good at the head of a

train of Bulleid's admirable post-war carriages. Many pleasant memories are revived of summer holiday excursions to the "Strong Country" when I see pictures of the engines in this state. I well recall the shock of seeing No. 35024 pounding through Wimbledon station in ex-works condition, in an experimental blue livery which was quickly adopted for the rest of the class. It looked quite smart on the air-smoothed casing, but (except for Pullmans) it clashed badly with the colour of the rolling stock. I could never raise much enthusiasm for their final livery of dark green, which seemed so unsuitable to their form when compared to Bulleid's original scheme.

It is not my intention to enter the debate on the pros and cons of Bulleid's engines in any detail, as a number of learned writers have already added much fuel to the fire in recent years, and no doubt there is more to come. My present work is presented to the reader as a straightforward pictorial survey of the various Bulleid engines in the many stages of their careers from delivery to withdrawal. As far as possible I have included the various detail alterations which took place over the years and I have used illustrations to emphasise these

Below: Equally successful was the appearance of the rebuilt Light Pacifics, as is well illustrated in this lovely view of 'Battle of Britain' Pacific No 34088 *213 Squadron* working the down 'Golden Arrow'; the train has just emerged from Knockholt Tunnel. /*Derek Cross*

Right: Once familiar sight as the crew prepared for the road. The fireman climbs to the footplate of rebuilt 'Battle of Britain' Pacific No 34087 *145 Squadron* at Weymouth shed. The engine was booked to work the Channel Islands Boat Train./*M. J. Esau*

points, which may be of particular help to railway modellers.

The book is divided into two main parts, the first dealing with Bulleid's designs for the Southern and for the CIE. The second part deals with the modification to the Pacifics undertaken by British Railways after Bulleid had left. Added to this are appendices dealing with diesel and electric locomotives, and one listing locomotive names. I would have liked to have added a further section, dealing with Bulleid's contribution to passenger carriage design, as this was an aspect of his work which produced some remarkable results. Even as I write today (1975) the Southern relies heavily upon suburban electric stock dating from the Bulleid era — which surely must have paid for itself time and time again since built.

I have already mentioned the move that Bulleid made from British Railways to the Irish National Rail system. This was in October 1949. Prior to this he had been involved with the Milne Report of 1948, which had examined the state of rail, road and canal transport in Eire for which Bulleid had been technical assessor.

Nearly seventy years of age and with no prospect for the continuation of his designs on the nationalised railways in Britain, O. V. S. Bulleid became Consulting Mechanical Engineer of CIE, and by February 1951 he had become CME, a position he held until May 1958 when he retired. This final phase of his railway career saw him as active as ever, as he modernised the CME's department and masterminded the changeover from steam to diesel traction.

In the pages that follow each of the Bulleid designs is dealt with in chronological order. It will be seen that his actual output was relatively small, when compared to the large numbers of locomotives of — for example — Stanier or Churchward. Whilst this is true, it must be acknowledged that Bulleid's contribution to the story of the British steam locomotive was exceptional. He took the classic Stephenson concept and attempted to improve upon it in a multitude of ways; if he failed in some cases this was as much the result of frustrations due to prevailing conditions (i.e. the outbreak of war or the nationalisation of the Southern Railway) as it was to technical inadequacy. In a nutshell,

Above left: The camera captures the blurred driving wheels of rebuilt 'Battle of Britain' class 4–6–2 No 34089 *602 Squadron* as the locomotive momentarily loses adhesion, leaving Waterloo with a train for Weymouth./*M. J. Esau*

Above: Steam departure. Rebuilt 'West Country' Pacific No 34018 *Axminster* makes a pleasing picture pulling out of Basingstoke with a Bournemouth train on 28 November 1964./*J. B. Wells*

Bulleid lived through the eleventh hour of British steam. The end was inevitable, but he did much to enliven the last of steam whilst the birth pangs of dieselisation were forced upon his reluctant attention.

In this, the fifth of a series of pictorial histories on the locomotives of British CMEs, I have once again had the invaluable and constant assistance of my dear friend Alec Swain. Many other people have heeded my requests for pictures and information and in particular I would like to thank the following: Colin Boocock; H. C. Casserley; L. Elsey; A. B. MacLeod; S. C. Nash; D. Piper; N. E. Preedy; Peter Rowledge and S. C. Townroe. The line drawings include two specially drawn by Peter Winding, who also gave much assistance on the choice of illustrations; other line drawings are reproduced by courtesy of the *Railway Gazette* and Ian Allan Library.

Brian Haresnape FRSA NDD
Box Hill, Surrey.
November 1975.

Bulleid Steam

New locomotives introduced by O. V. S. Bulleid for the Southern Railway and the CIE from 1941 to 1957.

4–6–2 Class MN (BR power class 8P*) Express Passenger Engines

Introduced: 1941
Total: 30
'Merchant Navy'

*Originally given as 7P

It was in March 1938 that the Southern Railway Board's authority was given for the construction of 10 new main-line steam locomotives of a new and, as yet undefined, design. Bulleid had outlined his task as the production of a locomotive capable of hauling trains of 550-600 tons at start-to-stop average speeds of 60 mph (on the Continental boat trains) and 70 mph (on the Western Section). As mentioned in the introduction he at first considered locomotives with eight-coupled driving wheels, but he finally settled for the 4–6–2 wheel arrangement, following objections from the Civil Engineer. If anyone at the time

Below: The drawing shows the original version of the 'Merchant Navy' class, with estimated weights, issued in 1941. The water filler for the tender is shown at the cab end, a feature later abandoned.

Bottom: Diagram issued in 1945, showing front end modifications and altered weights. It was only applicable to a few engines attached to the original tender design.

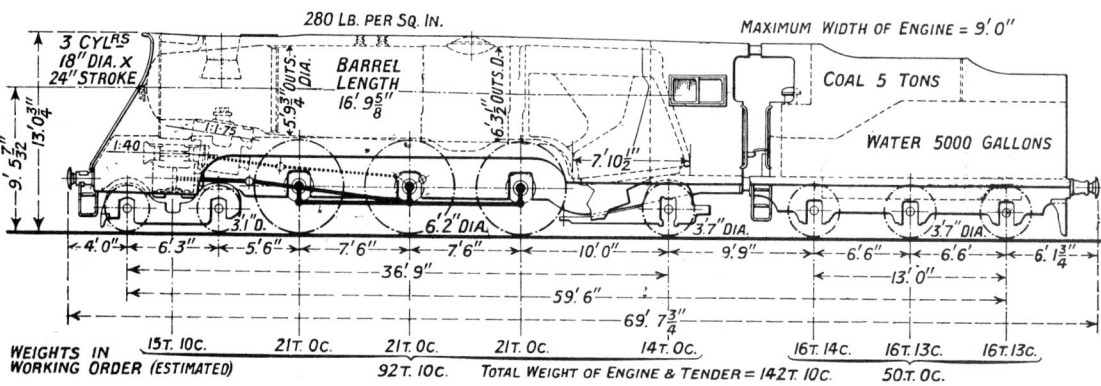

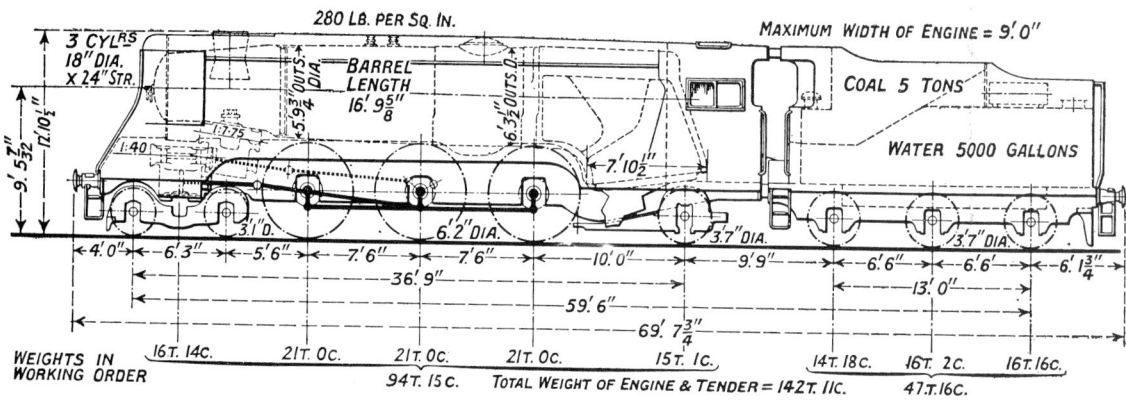

18

anticipated a Gresley-inspired Pacific adapted to Southern Railway requirements, their guess was to prove remarkably wide of the mark. Bulleid set about producing · a totally new design, with a number of quite novel aspects. In the course of time he showed himself capable of changing his mind – right up to the last minutes of design and construction – giving the drawing office staff a hectic time.

The outbreak of World War 2 overtook Bulleid in the midst of work on the first of the new engines, which did not appear until the early weeks of 1941. With a most unorthodox appearance, described as air-smoothed, (and intended to allow cleaning through carriage-washing plants) the new Pacific could hardly have been born at a more inopportune time.

Basically, the engine was a three-cylinder simple, with a novel chain-driven three-throw crank shaft operating valve gears for each cylinder and with an oil-bath, totally enclosing the sets of motion, located between the frames. Added to this breakaway from established practice was a whole host of new items, including patent Bulleid-Firth-Brown type wheels; clasp-type brakes; a boiler pressure of 280lb psi, welded steel firebox and thermic syphons. A wealth of labour-saving features ensured a ready welcome from railway shed

Above: The first 'Merchant Navy' engine, completed at Eastleigh in February 1941 and illustrated in as-built condition. The position of the numberplate and electric lights on the front end, above the bufferbeam, was quickly altered. The air-smoothed side casing was carried over the top and brought to a peak above the smokebox, with an air slot below. Livery was a matt finish Malachite green, with broad yellow lines, and the large brass castings used for name, number and ownership plates on both engine and tender had a red background. Wheel centres were also green, whilst the roof above the guttering was finished in matt black. A pivoting flat cap was provided on the roof to cover the chimney when the engine was 'cold', and the rear of the cab and tender front was roofed over, with flexible rubber bellows linking the two. The top of the casing on No 21C1 *Channel Packet* had a flat depression around the chimney area. The air intake to the chimney from the vertical front of the smokebox proved ineffective as a smoke-and-steam raiser. No 21C1 worked a 20coach test train from Eastleigh to Bournemouth and back on 22 February 1941 and was named *Channel Packet* at Eastleigh on 10 March 1941 by Lt. Col. J. T. C. Moore-Brabazon, then Minister of Transport./*Author's collection*

Left: Front end of No 21C1 *Channel Packet* in as-built condition, with front footstep on left-hand buffer only. Large cast brass ownership and number plates. Air intake above smokebox door, leading to the chimney./*Ian Allan Library*

Top: By June 1941 the teething troubles with No 21C1 had mounted to a stage where the engine was often seen on freight workings, a pattern which continued during 1942-3 with the rest of the first batch of ten engines, whilst efforts were made to eradicate the troubles. These troubles included excess weight and poor smoke clearance. Early detail modifications to the pioneer engine, seen here, included re-positioning of the front numberplate and electric lights, and provision of inset footholds on the sloping front below the smokebox. An order was issued that the class should be kept west of Salisbury until they were more satisfactory performers, and three of the Eastleigh design staff were sent to watch over them. There was persistent trouble with broken rocking-shafts and problems with the steel firebox, which

developed a tendency to crack. Two ex-LSWR locomotives, an A12 class 0–4–2 No 646 and an X6 class 4–4–0 No 657, were specially adapted to supply steam to Nos 21C1/2 whilst on shed, as it was intended to keep the Pacifics constantly in steam. At first there was one engine at Eastleigh and one at Salisbury; later both were at Salisbury./*Ian Allan Library*

Above: The second 'Merchant Navy', No 21C2 *Union Castle*, was completed at Eastleigh in June 1941. A noticeable modification was the enlarged air intake above the smokebox door, which exposed the flat sloping top of the smokebox (a feature of No 21C1 also, but one which was concealed by the casing.) This was applied to the remaining eight engines of the original batch, but still did not prove sufficient. The casing between the bufferbeam and front of the cylinders was cut away to expose the leading bogie wheel and there was a footstep and block on both buffers. Despite weight problems the large cast brass plates were retained./*British Rail*

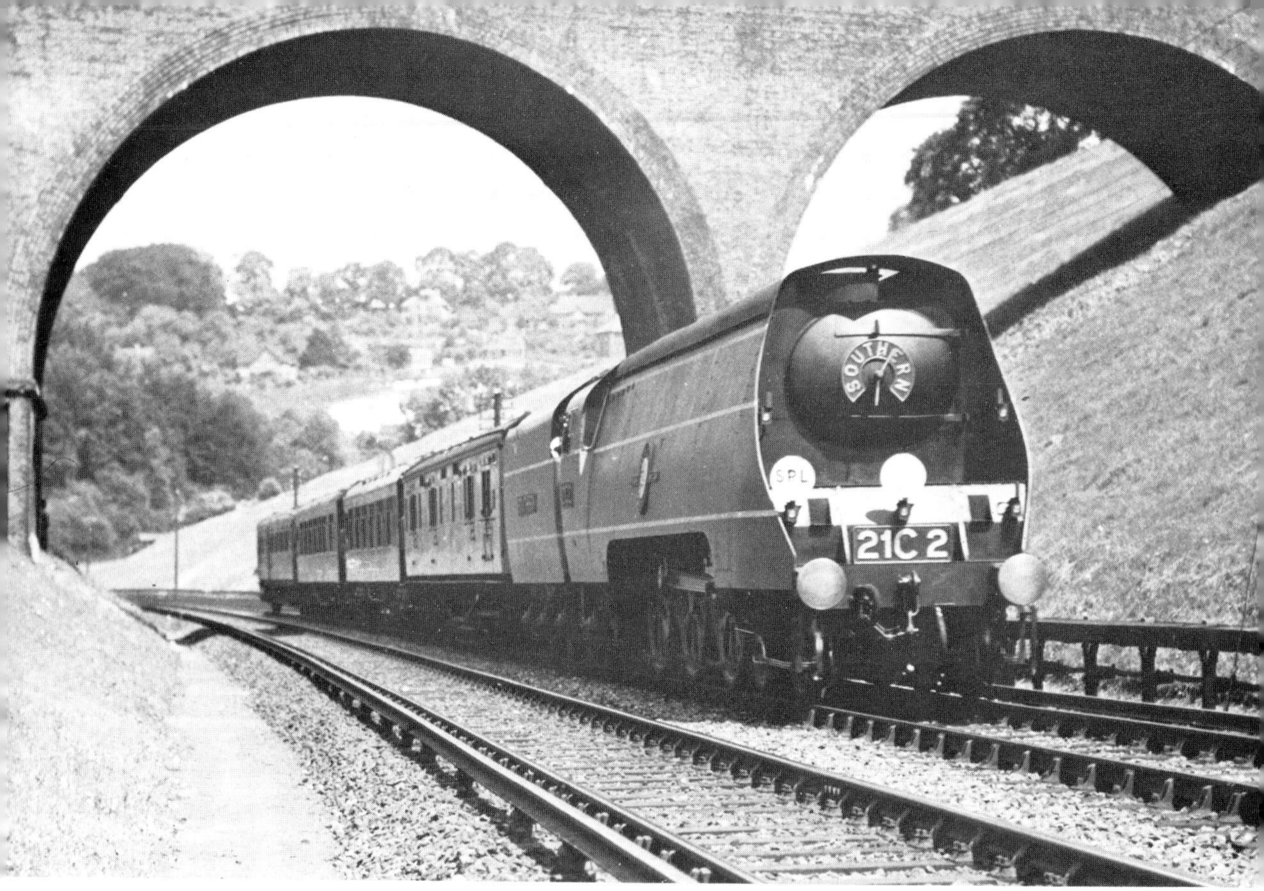
SOUTHERN
SPL
21C 2

SOUTHERN
ROYAL MAIL
MERCHANT NAVY CLASS
21C 3
SOUTHERN
21C 3

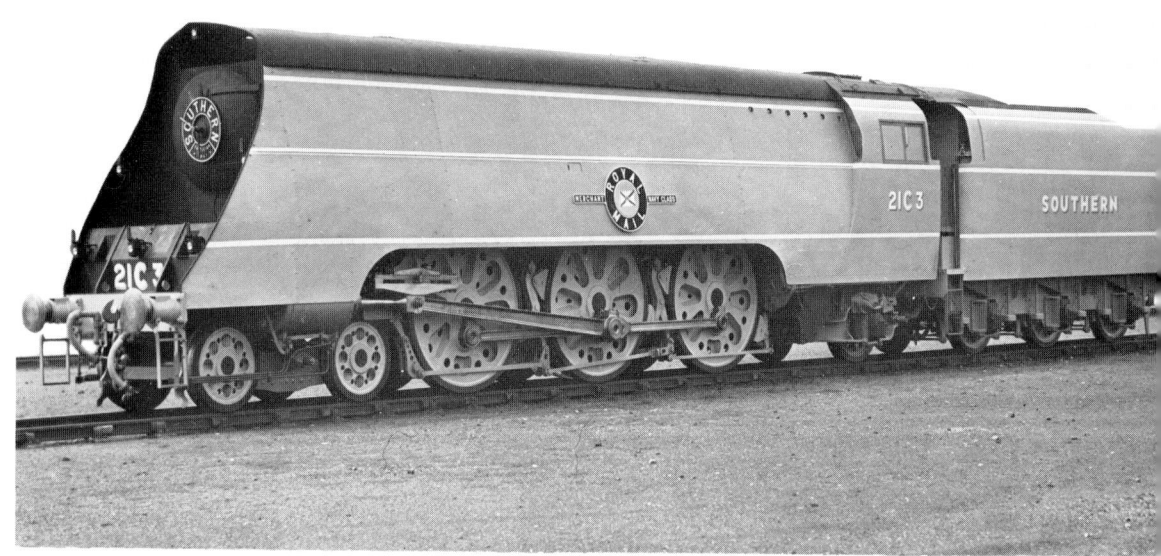

Left: Large painted number on the front, and additional date of building on the smokebox door plate, which no longer resembles the inverted horseshoe. Square hole round the chimney, with enlarged front slot. No 21C3 Royal Mail was photographed at Eastleigh on 21 October 1941, in the matt paint finish. Excess weight for the first two engines led to the decision not to fit the large metal numberplates to No 21C3, although these were in fact manufactured. To reduce the weight of Nos 21C1-5 holes were bored in the frames, and for Nos 21C6 onward lighter frames were constructed. /Ian Allan Library

Above left: This view of No 21C2 *Union Castle,* making a rare visit to the Brighton line with a four-car special at Merstham in July 1941, clearly shows the cut-away portion above the smokebox, exposing the multiple-jet chimney casing, which has a square hole surrounding it. On the return run the locomotive's valve gear failed at Streatham Common and the ensemble was hauled ignominiously by an ex LBSCR 13 class 4–4–2T for the remainder of the journey! /*Author's collection*

Left: Superstition among enginemen associated with the 'Merchant Navy' engines led to the alteration of the smokebox door ownership plate. Originally this resembled an inverted horseshoe (see previous illustrations of Nos 21C1/2), which was changed to a complete circle, with the place and date of building added below the word 'Southern'. No 21C3 *Royal Mail* displays this modification, together with the more serious abandonment of the cast brass numberplates and ownership plates on engine and tender – a move made to reduce weight. The main frames had lightening holes cut into them away from stress areas. No 21C3 was delivered from Eastleigh in September 1941 and was named at Waterloo on 24 October 1941. The tender water filler is visible in this illustration. /*Ian Allan Library*

staff, hard-pressed by the wartime conditions under which they then operated — until things began to go wrong.

The boiler was a magnificent affair, but it weighed too much (as did the valve motion) and economies had to be made in other parts to keep locomotive weight down to permissible levels. The boiler pressure was the highest that had ever been used in a British locomotive (other than in certain experimental designs). The boilers for the first 10 locomotives were built by the North British Locomotive Company, in Glasgow, as that famous firm had already considerable experience in the building of welded steel fireboxes — a feature chosen by Bulleid to reduce weight. The boiler barrel was tapered on the underside only and had a heating surface of 2176sq ft. The firebox (with combustion chamber) had 275sq ft including syphons, making a total evaporative surface of 2451sq ft. The superheater heating surface was 822sq ft, and the grate area of the wide firebox was $48\frac{1}{2}$sq ft. A multi-jet blast-pipe was fitted. In service these boilers proved to be magnificent steam producers.

The three cylinders were 18in diameter by 24in stroke, with the inside cylinder set at the very steep inclination of 1 in $7\frac{1}{2}$. With the intention of reducing the everyday maintenance routine of shed staff, Bulleid introduced his oil bath, which totally enclosed the valve motion, and which was meant to eliminate attention to the lubrication of the motion whilst the engine ran its entire span of service between works

Above: Wartime black livery for No 21C5 *Canadian Pacific,* photographed at Eastleigh Works in March 1942. The painted numerals on the front end are reduced in size. The locomotive was officially named at a ceremony held at Victoria Station, on 27 March 1942, by Mr. F. W. Mottley of the Canadian Pacific Railway Company, one of a number of such ceremonies held for the new engines, despite the stringent wartime attitudes then prevailing. From No 21C3 onward the cut away at the leading end of the tender sides was reduced in an effort to improve cab comfort. No 21C4 *Cunard White Star* was shot up by a German aircraft near Whimple in November 1942. The crew escaped injury and the engine was quickly repaired and returned to service./*Ian Allan Library*

Right: Minor changes were made in attempts to improve smoke deflection, with little or no effect, and in a determined effort to improve matters Bulleid placed the problem with Southampton University. A wooden scale model of a 'Merchant Navy' was constructed at Lancing Carriage works and sent to the University's wind tunnel. As a result of these experiments, in which the flow of air was studied, the front end of No 21C10 *Blue Star* was modified as shown. Similar modifications were made to Nos 21C8/9. The casing above the smokebox was brought forward in a lip, or cowl, and the sides were cut into to form individual side wings. A considerable improvement was observed in tests using a ciné camera located behind the driver's cab front window, although the design was criticised because it further restricted the view forward. A compromise solution was reached, with the top cowling separate from the side deflectors, which were flattened to reduce the overall width at the smokebox end./*Ian Allan Library*

overhauls. This oil bath had a capacity of no less than 40 gallons and included reversible gear pumps, chain driven from the valve crankshaft, to lift oil from the sump through pipes, and distribute it over the moving parts. It proved impossible to prevent leakage of oil and in some cases outbreaks of fire occurred when the oil soaked into the boiler lagging.

The design of the valve gear itself was to allow for this total enclosure in the oil bath, set between the main frames. The space available was relatively small. Bulleid's intention was to create a locomotive with its parts running in oil – like his car. This scheme was drawn-up before the war using a chain drive, without conventional valve spindles. Quite late in the day he considered using an improved Caprotti gear, but perhaps Bulleid foresaw the problems of wartime production, as it was the patent chain-driven radial gear which he finally adopted for his new Pacifics. He fitted a steam-operated reverser, and it was the poor performance of this latter feature, together with the valve gear, which was to cause so much trouble in everyday service, until the modifications made by BR eliminated both causes (see pages 78-89.)

The spacing of the frames was closer than normal, with the centres of the horn cheeks in line with them. The first two engines were too heavy and holes were cut, in the frames, to lighten them; later engines of the first batch of 10 had these alterations from new. The massive cast steel frame stretchers were also reduced in weight as much as possible. Another method of reducing the overall weight of the locomotives (which had proved to be 90.15

Above: No 21C16, delivered in March 1945 in austere black livery and seen here working a down West of England express near Hook. The second batch of ten engines, Nos 21C11-20, were delivered between December 1944 and June 1945 in preparation for peacetime and had numerous detail changes compared to the initial ten. As built, they had short, flat smoke deflectors, set at a slope, and the front-end side valances were shortened, with a modified inward curve to the bufferbeam. The cutaway to expose the coupled wheels was more angular and there were modifications to the cab and tender contours. The side sheets of the cab were turned inwards to give added protection to the crew, and windows were let into them. The tender side sheets were similarly treated, and a 'tunnel' ran between the coal space and the tender sides, giving the crew a better rearward vision, also providing housing for the fireirons. The middle lamp irons were relocated, on the smokebox door, instead of on the inside front edge of the smoke deflectors. */M. W. Earley*

Right: The pioneer Bulleid Pacific, No 21C1 *Channel Packet* was selected to work the inaugural trip of the 'Golden Arrow' Pullman train, when it was restored on 13 April 1946 with the return to peacetime conditions. In the latter days of World War 2 the locomotive had run in plain black livery, but had retained the cast brass name and number plates – somewhat surprisingly – and these plates remained when Eastleigh outshopped No 21C1 in full Malachite green livery – certainly a sight for sore eyes after the drab war years. The front end had an interim modification, following the experiments with No 21C10, the side casing was pressed out to form small deflectors with a cowl above the smokebox on which the top electric light was located. A footstep was added to the right-hand buffer, but the curved cowling was retained between bufferbeam and cylinders. The effect of a glossy varnish finish to the livery makes an interesting comparison with the original matt finish applied to Nos 21C1-3 when new (see pages 19-22)./*Ian Allan Library*

Above: Another view of No 21C16 *Elders and Fyffes*, taken at Salisbury when still in plain black livery in 1945. The more angular style of the air-smoothed casing is emphasised, also the very short smoke deflectors, which ended in line with the rear of the cylinders. The tender is of 5 100gal capacity and has brackets attached to the spring ends, instead of the link hangers used on the tenders of Nos 21C1-10. The side wings of the coal space are brought further forward, and a steam heat pipe is visible below the side of the tank./*P. F. Winding*

Top right: Three 'Merchant Navy' Pacifics were selected to take part in the historic Interchange Trials of 1948, Nos 35017/19/20 (formerly 21C17/19/20,) and for these trials they were temporarily fitted with LMS tenders (with water scoops) which were unfortunately painted black. No 35020 was held in reserve on the Southern and was not in fact used. The other two locomotives put up some terrific performances during the trials. No 35017 ran on the London Midland and Eastern Regions, whilst No 35019 ran on the Western. For trials on the Southern No 35018 was selected, attached to its normal tender. No 35019 *French Line C.G.T.* is seen here leaving Paddington on the 1.30 pm to Plymouth on the first day of the trials./*F. R. Hebron*

Right: Although renumbered into the BR system, with the unique Bulleid notation replaced by Gill Sans numerals, No 35014 (formerly 21C14) *Nederland Line*, was still in SR Malachite green livery devoid of any signs of ownership, *circa* 1949. The smoke deflector wing plates had been extended rearwards and the cab front had been modified, with a wedge shape to the upper part. The slidebars were encased in an attempt to prevent sand reaching them, which was not successful, and eventually the front sanding gear was removed. The air-smoothed casing over the cylinders and forward to the bufferbeam was painted black./*J. H. Aston*

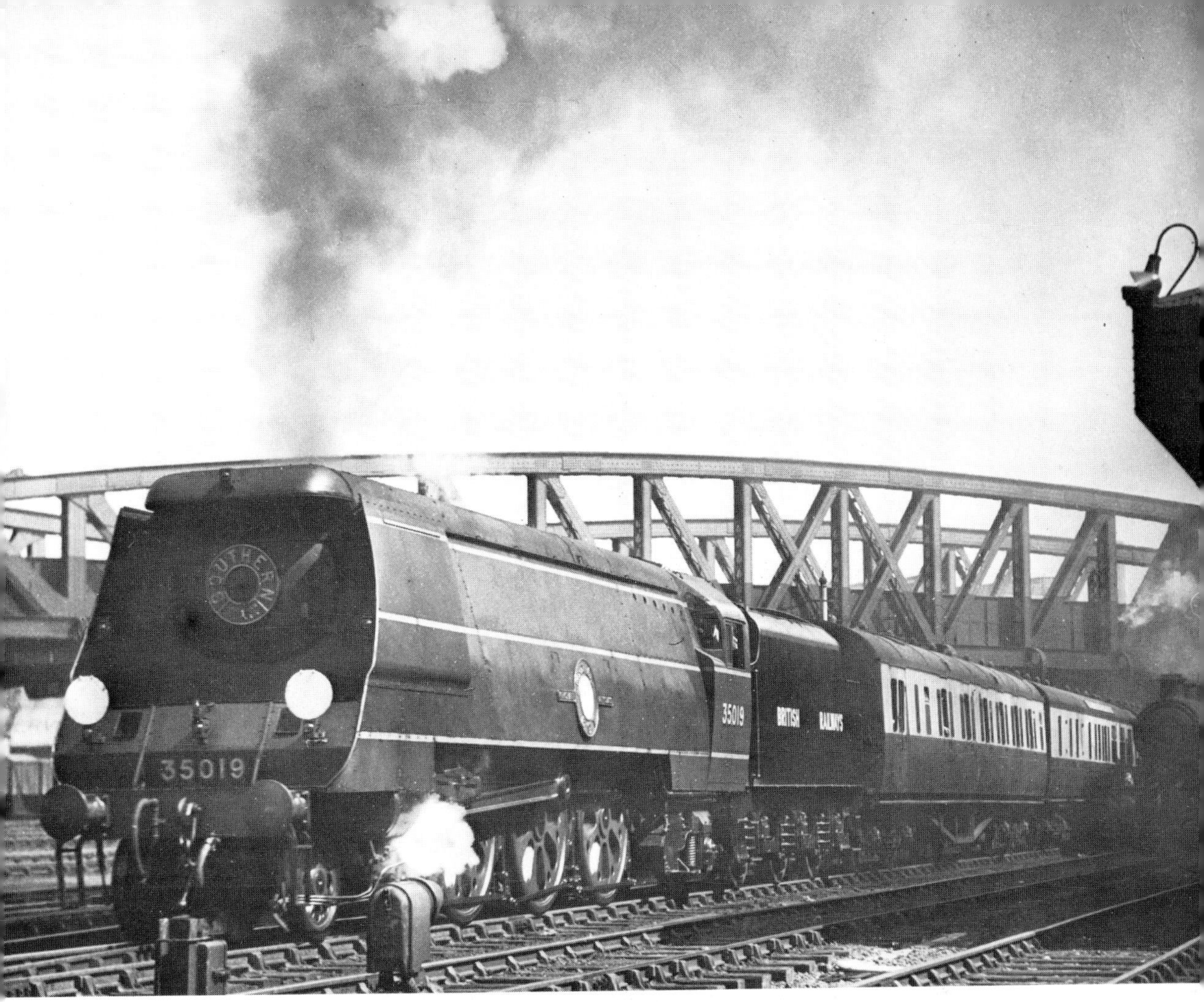
SOUTHERN
35019
35019
BRITISH RAILWAYS

35014
35014

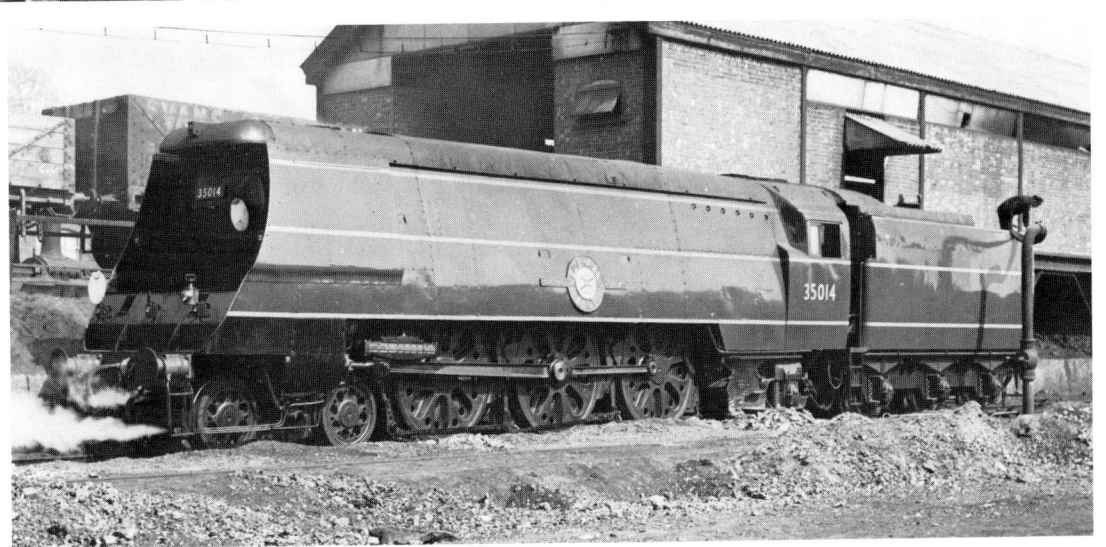

tons empty) was the use of thinner sheeting for the air-smoothed casing and the cab sides. The empty weight was reduced to 86.55tons, or 96.3tons in full working order. The ornamental cast brass numberplates on cabsides and front and the large cast 'Southern' plates on the tender were also removed, to reduce weight, and were replaced by painted letters and numerals.

The BFB (Bulleid-Firth-Brown) wheels were a patent variation on the box type, and had the advantage of greater and more continuous support for the tyre. The coupled wheel diameter was 6ft 2in, the leading bogie was 3ft 1in and the trailing axle had 3ft 7in diameter wheels. This latter axle was carried by a trailing truck of the 'delta' type. No reciprocating balance weights were used for the coupled driving wheels, but weights were inserted in the wheel rims in respect of rotating weights.

A considerable amount of attention was given by Bulleid to providing greater comfort and ease of operation, from the enginemen's viewpoint. In particular he provided electric lighting, worked from a steam generator. This illuminated the headcode lamps at the front of the engine and the rear of the tender, inspection

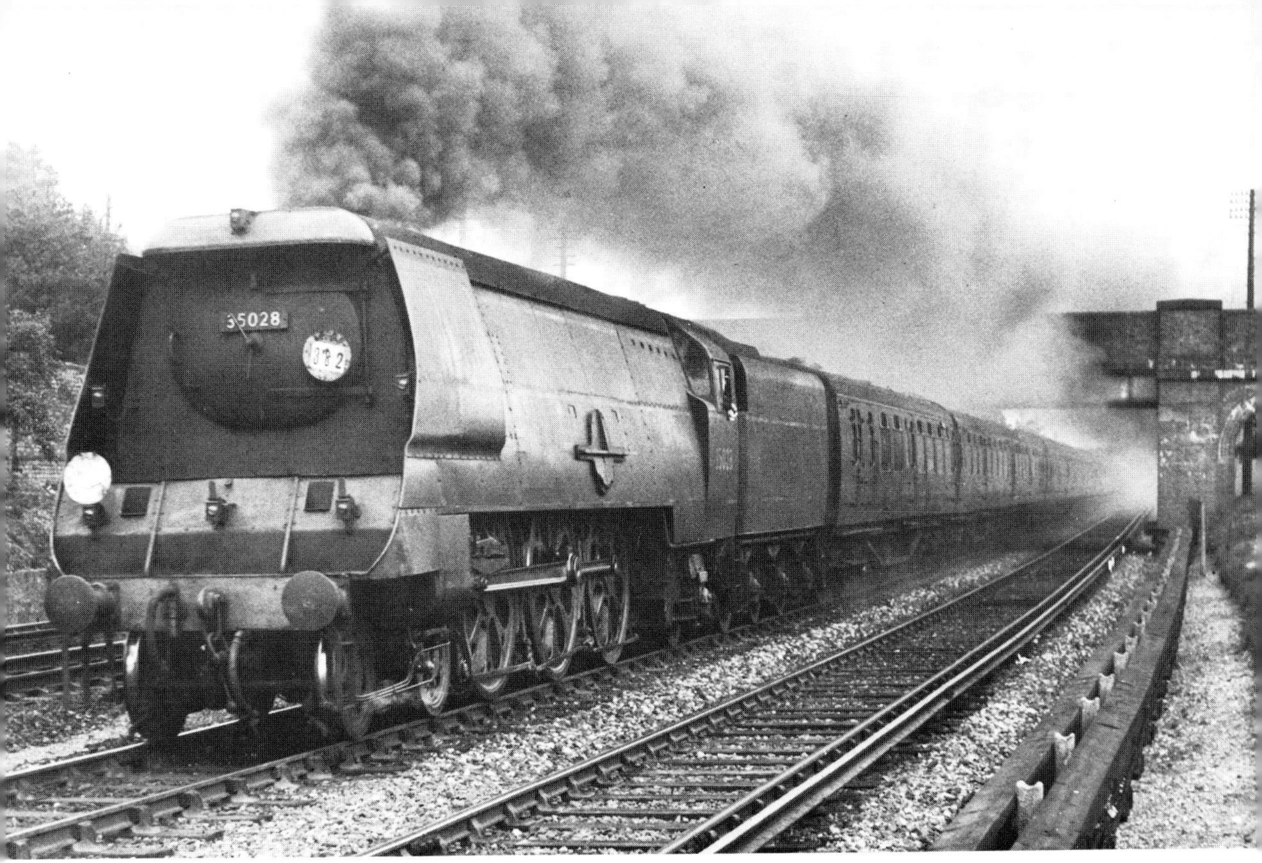
35028

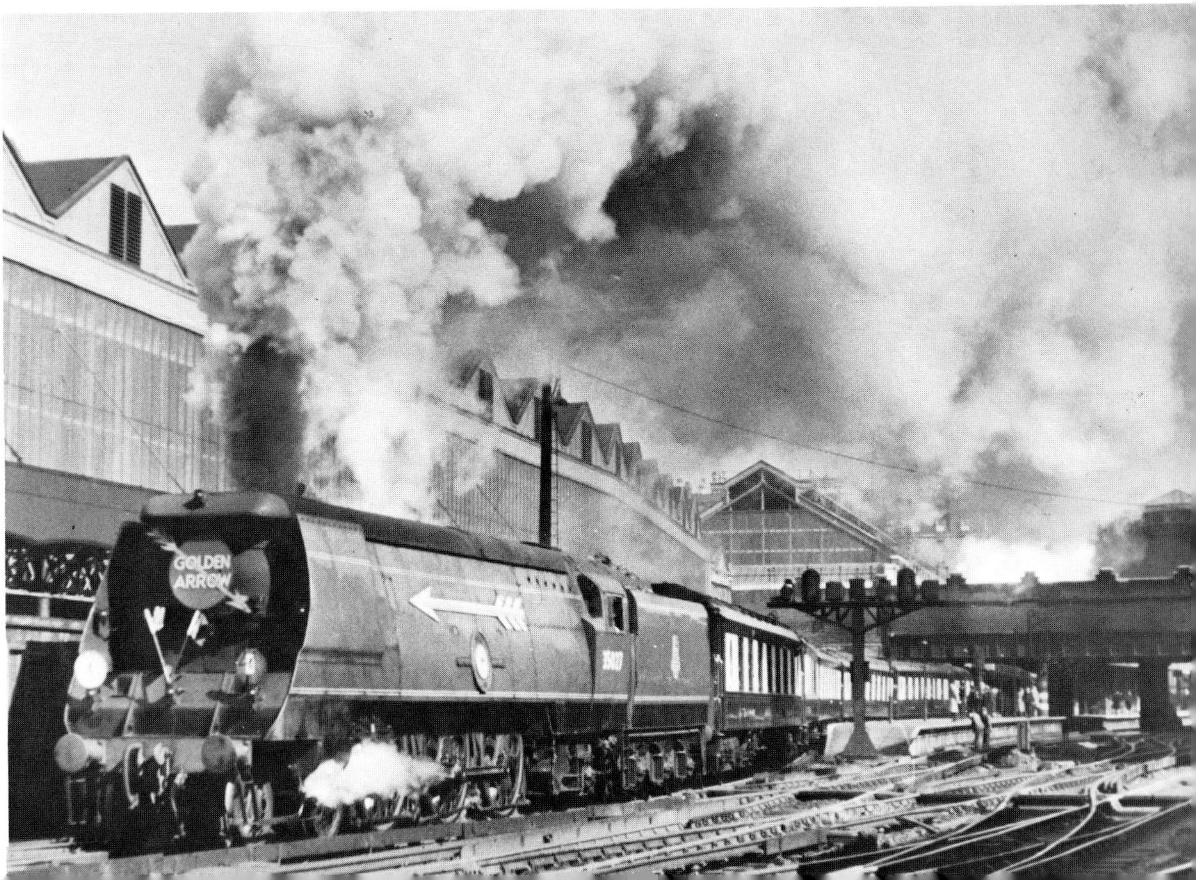
GOLDEN
ARROW

lights under the casing and above the wheels, and also the cab interior and fittings; a light below the footplate allowed the fireman to check the working of the injectors at night. The layout of the cab was revised from previous SR practice and the grouping of controls for both driver and fireman was altered to allow both men to perform their duties without getting in each other's way. Steam-operated firedoors were fitted, as in contemporary American practice.

The six-wheeled tender was of welded construction and the profile of the sides matched that of the post-war Bulleid carriages. The first tender had an array of footsteps and grab handles on the rear, later replaced by tubular steel ladders, and there were tank fillers on each side at the cab end, as well as in the normal position on top at the back. Water capacity was 5000gal and coal capacity 5tons for the first 10 tenders, which weighed 50tons in working order.

Right: A bizarre combination of blue-liveried tender coupled to green-liveried engine, seen on No 35002 *Union Castle* at Nine Elms shed on 22 March 1952. The engine still had the original cab design although the front end had been up-dated with smoke deflectors and trough. The tender illustrates the elaborate ladders and six electric lights which were developed by Bulleid (the original design on No 21C1 had only grab rails and footsteps, no ladders). Also visible are the bearing springs with link hangers, a feature of the first 10 tenders. The blue livery was abandoned in May 1951, and the first 'Merchant Navy' to appear in the standard dark green was No 35024./*C. G. Geard*

Above: Extra smoke deflection area on No 35020 *Bibby Line,* with a rearward extension to the plates (similar to modifications tried out on a few 'West Country' Pacifics; see pages 56-65). The engine is in blue livery and was photographed working the down 1.00pm Waterloo-Ilfracombe express, near Worting Junction on 4 August 1951. This engine was working the 4.30pm from Exeter Central on 24 April 1953, when the driving axle fractured as the train was accelerating downhill through Crewkerne. By good fortune the engine remained on the rails and no one was injured, but the incident was serious enough to require the temporary withdrawal of the entire class, whilst an examination was made of the driving axles. To cover the power shortage the Southern borrowed locomotives from other Regions, including some Gresley V2s, and Stanier 'Black Fives.'/*E. D. Bruton*

With a tractive effort of 37 500lb at 85per cent of boiler pressure the new Pacifics were certainly powerful machines and despite a number of persistent teething troubles they could run freely, although restricted to the Salisbury – Exeter line (1942-44). Another 10 were ordered, which had a number of differences, and which weighed more, at 94¾ tons in full working order. In particular the boiler was altered. Whereas the first 10 boilers, built at Glasgow, had the front ring of the barrel tapered on the underside and the rear ring parallel, the last 20 boilers built (at Eastleigh) together with five spare boilers, had the front ring parallel and the rear ring tapered along the bottom, which had the effect of reducing weight and water capacity, but not the heating surface. The layout of the sanding gear was altered (see page 95) and there were improvements to the design of the cab and tender. Other detail alterations are shown in the accompanying illustrations.

A third, and final, batch of 10 'Merchant Navy' Pacifics emerged in the early days of nationalisation, and never carried the odd Bulleid numbering system – becoming instead BR Nos 35021-30. These had further detail alterations, including modified cabs and longer smoke deflectors and were fitted from new with TIA water treatment apparatus. These were given 6000gal tenders (in most cases they at

Above: In the 1950s a close study was still being made of the performance of modern steam locomotives and one aid to this was the self-weighing tender, which allowed an accurate record to be kept of fuel consumption in everyday service, as well as trial running or testing. Locomotives on each Region were selected to run with self-weighing tenders, and the Southern fitted a 6000gal version to No 35018 in 1952. The revised style of lining-out for the BR green livery, together with the small emblem, did not really match the engine. The tender carried TIA (Trâitement Intégrale Armand) water treatment equipment, with the tank visible on the rear end of the tender, alongside the vacuum reservoirs. The TIA scheme was applied to the last ten engines, Nos 35021-30, when new, and gradually extended to the rest of the class./*L. Elsey*

Left: No 35019 *French Line C.G.T.* was fitted with a single blastpipe and normal diameter chimney, in 1951, under the auspicies of R. G. Jarvis. The engine is seen arriving at Salisbury one hot noonday in July 1953. From this angle, the tunnel between the tender sides and the coal space is clearly visible. Another modification introduced by Jarvis, after Bulleid had left the Southern, was the lowering of the boiler pressure from 280 to 250lb psi. All but eight of the class were so treated before the rebuilding programme commenced in 1956. The single chimney was not adopted, however, and No 35019 reverted to the multiple-jet arrangement for the remainder of her career, including the final rebuilt form. Another experiment was undertaken at this time, when No 35014 was fitted with a boiler without thermic syphons./*G. F. Heiron*

first ran with borrowed 5500gal tenders) and the forward water filling points were not fitted. On this last batch of engines the trailing truck frame was of fabricated steel plate, instead of the one-piece steel casting previously used, in order to reduce weight.

The engines were built as follows:

Nos 21C1-21C10	Eastleigh	1941/2
Nos 21C11-21C20	Eastleigh	1944/5
Nos 35021-35030	Eastleigh	1948/9

Nos 21C1-21C20 were renumbered 35001-35020 by British Railways, in 1948.

Despite many modifications after No 21C1 appeared in 1941, it was apparent to the men on the ground that many of the features which were intended to ease their job did precisely the opposite. The oil bath, the valve motion, the steam reverser and the difficulties of access created by the air-smoothed casing, all contributed to costly and excessive maintenance when compared to more conventional steam designs of equivalent size and power. An early step taken by BR was the reduction of the boiler pressure from 280 to 250lb psi which had the effect of reducing their tendency to chronic bouts of slipping. In any case, the footplatemen tended to run the engines quite happily at less than the 280lb.

Inevitably, the case for modification won the day, thereby bringing the engines more into line with contemporary BR standard practice, by removing the more unorthodox features. The subsequent history of the 'Merchant Navy' Pacifics in their modified form is described in, Section 6, on pages 78 - 89, including dates of rebuilding and withdrawal, and a list of examples preserved.

Above: By 1955 the self-weighing tender had been attached to No 35014 *Nederland Line,* seen here at Eastleigh on 9 April 1955, after attention at the works. The livery scheme has lost the original simplicity, with the cab sides lined to match the tender rather than the sides of the boiler. The picture makes an interesting comparison with the view of the same engine reproduced on page 27. The casing ahead of the cylinders has been removed, giving a more angular appearance to the front end, and the forward sanding gear has been removed together with the protective cover over the slidebars./*F. Gamblin*

Above right: In November 1956, No 35010 *Blue Star,* was stored at Bournemouth Central awaiting removal to Eastleigh for rebuilding. This was the first of the initial ten members of the class to be selected for rebuilding; all previous examples had been from the later 20 engines. During rebuilding of No 35010 it proved necessary to renew the main frames ahead of the cylinders. As seen here the locomotive illustrates the final condition of the early Bulleid Pacifics, with revised cab design, smoke deflectors and trough, and air-smoothed casing removed ahead of the cylinders. The tender is still in basically original state. No 35010 emerged from Eastleigh in rebuilt form in January 1957, and by October 1959 all 30 engines were dealt with, the last two being Nos 35006/28. This view of No 35010 clearly illustrates the curved cutaway of the air-smoothed casing, above the driving wheels; a feature of the first ten engines, also the horizontal rib midway down the casing (introduced on Nos 21C3-10.)./*C. P. Boocock*

Centre right: Additional train nameboards were attached to the smoke deflectors for the locomotive working the 'Devon Belle' Pullman, finished in red and yellow. With a light load of five cars, plus the observation car at the rear, 'Merchant Navy' No 35021 *New Zealand Line* is seen at Winchfield on 13 July 1957. The engine is attached to a rebuilt tender, although not itself converted until two years later. In fact modification of the tenders was commenced in 1952, with removal of the raves to allow easier access for water filling./*M. W. Earley*

Left: One of the last 'Merchant Navy' Pacifics to be rebuilt was the pioneer No 35001 *Channel Packet* and in the interim period it was attached to a rebuilt tender for service on the Eastern Section, to which it returned in 1957. The engine is seen working a down Belgian Boat Express near Ashford in the August of that year, with a Class L 4–4–0 on the adjacent track. Comparison with the picture of No 35001 (as 21C1) on page 19, clearly shows the extent of the modifications since 1946, in particular to the front end and the cab. *Channel Packet* was rebuilt at Eastleigh in August 1959. The subsequent careers of the rebuilt 'Merchant Navy' Pacifics forms the content of Section 6, on pages 78-89./*P. Ransome-Wallis*

0–6–0 Class Q1 (BR power class 5F)
Goods Engines
Introduced: 1942
Total: 40
'Austerity'

The final locomotive design produced by R. E. L. Maunsell before his retirement was a modest 0–6–0 derived mainly from existing standard parts, and intended for use on certain lines where weight restrictions had meant the prolonged retention of pre-Grouping types, such as the LSWR Beattie and SER Stirling goods engines. This new Maunsell class Q was in the pipeline when Bulleid arrived on the Southern, and he is reported to have regretted the fact that he arrived too late to have building halted. He categorised them as pedestrian and nondescript for a design produced as late as 1938.

Circumstances were to change drastically in a short space of time, with the outbreak of World War 2, and O. V. S. Bulleid was presented with a traffic requirement for an 0–6–0 locomotive to be capable of operating the heavier loads of wartime over the same secondary routes as the Maunsell Q, which had a total weight of less than 54 tons for the engine. As Bulleid himself explained at a talk to Feltham enginemen in November 1942, the easiest course would have been to build a further 40 Qs, but experience with the existing engines had shown that the motion and cylinder design left something to be desired, and the boiler capacity was somewhat less than

Right: Photographed just before the final coat of black paint was applied; newly completed 0–6–0 No C1 outside Brighton Works. An interesting deviation from the finalised livery is evident in the very high position of the lettering on the tender. At this stage the numerals and lettering were on metal plates attached to the engine. The lack of running-plate emphasised the BFB wheels, which were about 10 per cent lighter than the conventional spoked type. The locomotive frame was lightened wherever possible, and fabricated details were used instead of steel castings. Essentially an austerity design, Bulleid intended it to have a relatively short life, with a minimum of overhaul. In fact, the class was destined to operate for some 26 years!/*British Rail*

Below right: Nothing quite like No C1 had been delivered from a British locomotive works before, and the emergence of Bulleid's new concept of the classic 0–6–0 maid-of-all-work, in the midst of war, provoked an immediate outcry from enthusiasts who were shocked by the apparent disregard for aesthetic appearance. The first of the class is seen here in as-built condition, at Brighton on 26 March 1942 in plain black livery with yellow lettering shaded in green. The tender, which was largely of welded construction, was similar to the 'Merchant Navy' Pacific's design, but had the bearing springs attached to brackets (later also applied to the Pacific version.) The tender cab was linked by rubber bellows, at roof level, to the engine cab. Both live-steam injectors were mounted on the fireman's side. Tender capacity was 3700gal and 5tons of coal, with the coal space designed to be self-trimming. /*British Rail*

Below: Q1 class 0–6–0, as built.

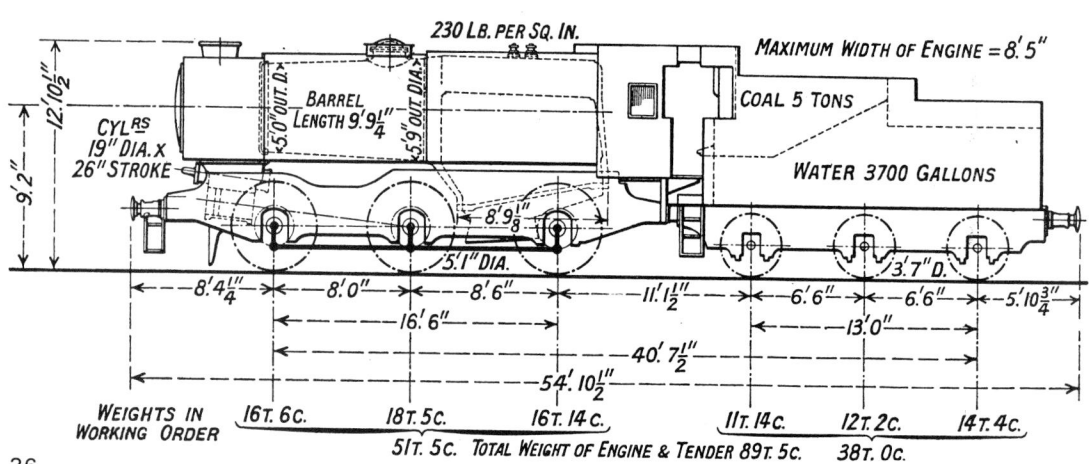

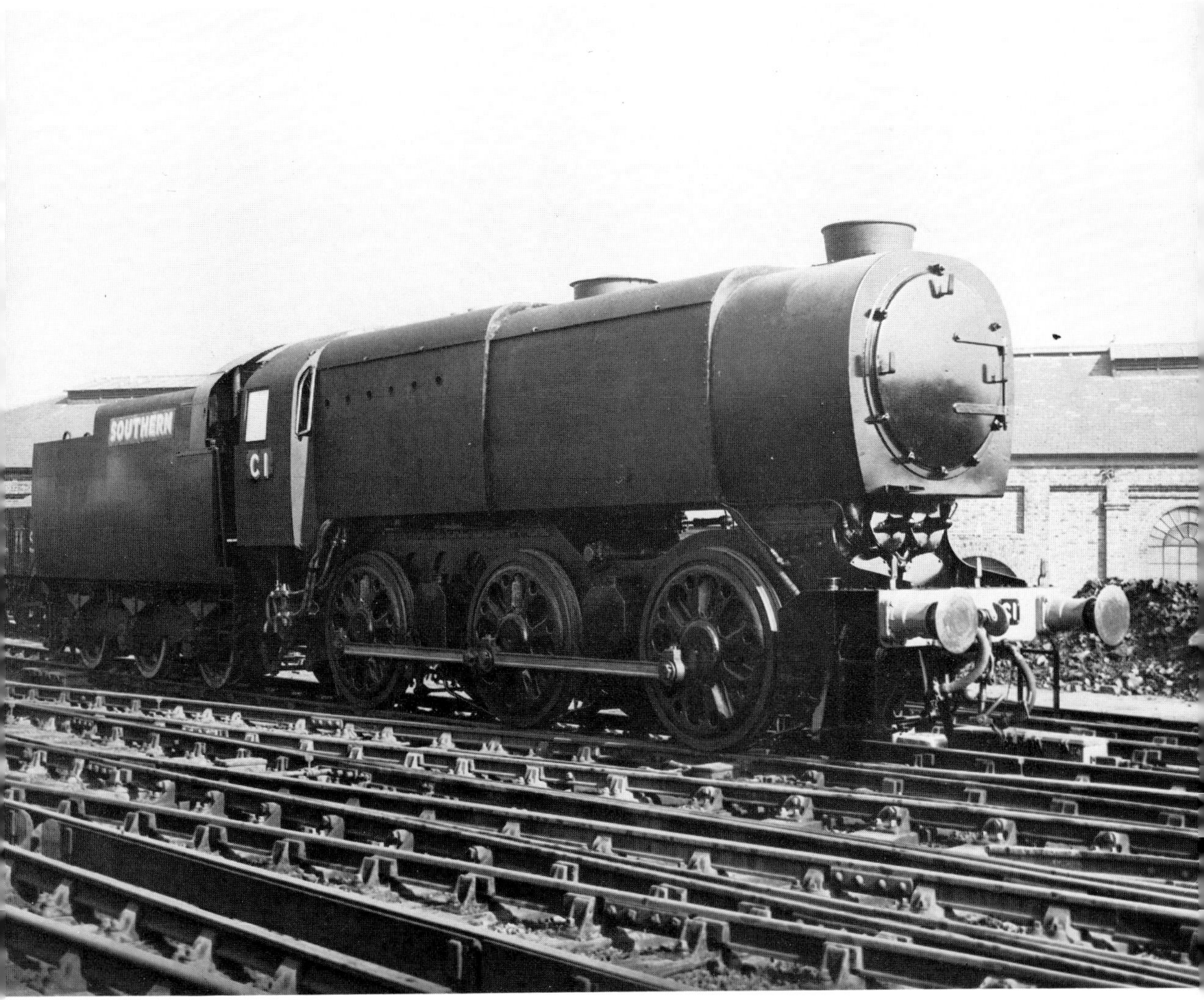
SOUTHERN
C1

SOUTHERN
C1

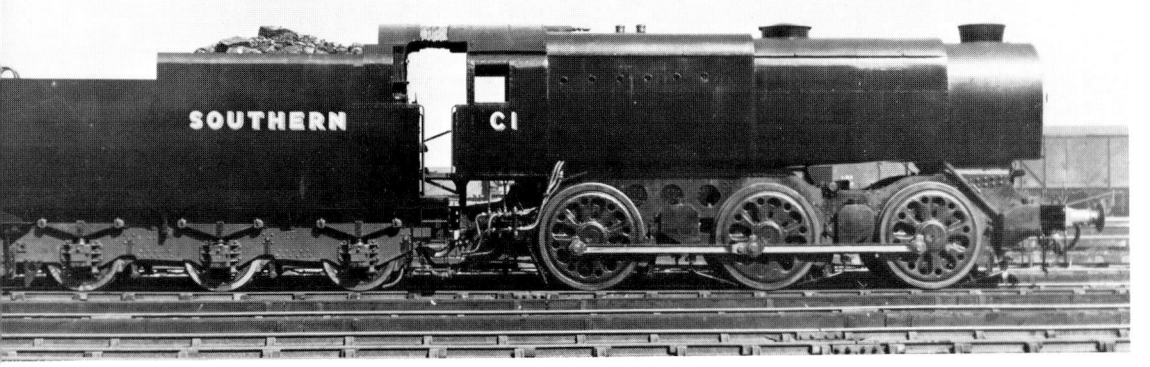

Far left: Unlike the Pacifics, the new 0–6–0s were not fitted with electric lighting and there was a noticeable lack of handrails at the front end. A curious and unnecessary ornamentation of No C1 was the small plate at first attached to the bufferbeam, which displayed the locomotive number on a black background. Provision of a steam heating hose was largely to allow their use on empty coaching stock workings./*British Rail SR*

Left: Tender end detail of 0–6–0 No C1, taken at Brighton on 27 February 1942, showing very well the clean and simple layout and welded construction. Vacuum cylinders are located below bufferbeam, to the rear of the rear axle./*British Rail SR*

Below: Class Q1 0–6–0 No C21 is seen heading a down goods near Winchester in 1948. The lettering 'Southern' on the tender is now centrally placed and grab rails have been added to the smokebox door, and surround. The locomotive number is painted directly on to the bufferbeam. A sliding shutter has been added to the cutaway at the leading end of the tender, which gave access to the tank fillers./*Donovan E. H. Box*

the new traffic demands required; he therefore set his sights higher.

In peacetime conditions the Southern was primarily a passenger-carrying line and therefore possessed a large number of passenger and mixed-traffic locomotives which, although allowed over many of the secondary routes which were suddenly the focus of wartime goods traffic, were deficient in power for wartime needs. Thus was born the idea of Bulleid's second locomotive for the Southern Railway, an Austerity 0–6–0 with the largest boiler that could be accommodated on the chassis, and with the weight kept to the minimum by frugal design. The Q1 class had a high tractive effort, of 30 000lb (compared to the 26 157lb of the Maunsell Q class engines) and yet could operate over all but 7 per cent of SR routes.

To achieve this remarkable version of the classic British 0–6–0 maid-of-all-work, Bulleid went back to basic principles in design, doing away with all unnecessary ornamentation and dispensing with a number of customary features. Because of the war it was not possible to obtain generous allocations of steel for

locomotive construction, so in order to keep the weight down to the required figure he departed from convention in locomotive appearance and produced a 'bare' apparition which had the more conservative students of British steam locomotive design in an uproar.

The firebox was based on that of the Maunsell 'Lord Nelson' class and the same press blocks were used for the throat-plate and back-plate as for that class, which was in itself a useful economy. The grate area of 27sq ft was the largest of any British 0–6–0. The boiler barrel was in one piece, tapered equally on top and bottom from 5ft 9in to 5ft outside – dimensions which were the largest size consistent with providing the driver with a good look-out that came within the loading gauge requirement. The length of the barrel, 9ft $9\frac{1}{4}$in, was dictated by the length of the firebox. The total heating surface was 1860sq ft, with the firebox providing 170sq ft, the tubes and flues 1472-sq ft and the superheater 218sq ft. The boiler pressure at 230lb was high for an 0–6–0 and tractive effort was, as stated earlier, 30 000lb at 85 per cent boiler pressure.

The revolutionary exterior finish was partly

governed by the need to reduce weight, as already explained, but also partly to simplify manufacture. The boiler lagging was a product known as Idaglass, and in order that this should not bear any weight the boiler casing was carried directly on the frames, instead of embracing the barrel. Two brackets supported the casing, which was in two sections. The traditional running boards above the wheels were dispensed with, saving 17cwt, and the boiler casing was squared-off at the lower edge to create rudimentary splashers for the coupled wheels. The smokebox was shaped so as to provide a greater volume than the largest circular one which could have been fitted, also leaving more room for maintenance and repair procedures. The upper shape of the smokebox was echoed in the shape of the two sections of boiler casing, producing a distinctive contour. The five-nozzle multiple-jet blastpipe was provided with a basic stovepipe chimney and the dome cover was similarly lacking in ornamentation. The two inside cylinders, of 19in diameter by 26in stroke, had overhead piston valves with outside admission operated by Stephenson link

Above left: An early example of renumbering in the BR scheme was No 33033 (formerly C33), which at first had SR type numerals on the cabsides and no emblem or lettering on the tender. It carried this style as late as 26 September 1953 when photographed at Ashford Shed, with smokebox freshly painted. Throughout their careers the Q1 0–6–0s were always in plain black livery; only the lettering and insignia varied in design. The Bulleid numbering scheme was replaced by BR in 1948, when Nos C1-C40 became Nos 33001-40. */R. E. Vincent*

Above: Hauling ballast for sea wall repairs, Q1 0–6–0 No 33007 makes a fine sight as she climbs the 1 in 100 up from Herne Bay. When new, the pioneer engine No C1 worked a trial trip over the 24miles from Woking to Basingstoke with a mixed train of approximately 1000tons, taking 58min without extending the locomotive. The booked time for 800tons was then 66min. */P. Ransome-Wallis*

motion, giving a maximum travel of $6\frac{7}{8}$in; the reversing gear was steam-operated. The cast steel box wheels were of the same Bulleid-Firth-Brown patent type as introduced with the 'Merchant Navy' Pacifics, and had a diameter of 5ft 1in. The wheelbase was the same as for the Q class (see diagram) and the cylinders were in the same position.

To quote Bulleid's own words: 'The result was an engine having a light weight of only 45tons 18cwt. By fabricating and the use of thin plates, the weight of the tender was reduced to 16tons. An engine and tender of normal design would be about 14tons heavier, so on 40 engines 560tons of weight has been saved. This is equal to about 700tons of raw materials, equal to nine more engines and tenders. And the completed engine complied with the Engineer's limitations'.

The engines were built as follows:

Nos C1-C16	Brighton	1942
Nos C17-C36	Ashford	1942
Nos C37-C40	Brighton	1942

The 1946 locomotive building programme for the Southern Railway included a further 20 0-6-0 locomotives. These did not come to fruition, but some material was ordered for parts, and the early schemes for the 'Leader' class (see page 66) were intended to make use of these parts, although the final design did not in fact incorporate them. In his post-war plan for standard locomotives Bulleid did not include the Q1 0-6-0s, partly because of their somewhat restricted brake power on unfitted

Above: Cross-London transfer freights were one of the duties performed by the Q1 0-6-0s, and during World War 2 they hauled some remarkable loads for their size. In BR days No 33013 was photographed passing Graham Road signalbox with a westbound transfer freight, on 21 March 1959. In the background an Eastern Region Class N7 0-6-2T can be seen passing overhead with a Liverpool Street-Enfield Town train, approaching Hackney Downs station./*K. L. Cook*

Above right: An eleven-coach train of Western Region stock forms the Hastings-Birmingham relief train, seen passing Cooksbridge in the charge of No 33036 on 6 August, 1960. The Q1s proved themselves capable of a fair turn of speed on such passenger duties, up to 75 mph, although the enginemen were not enamoured of the spectacle of the side rods (clearly visible from the cab) in motion at such times, due to the lack of a footplate or splashers, and rain water was thrown up, restricting forward vision by forcing the driver to take cover!/*S. C. Nash*

freights. Nevertheless, the 40 engines built proved themselves most worthy members of the motive power stud, and perhaps over the years one even became accustomed to their unorthodox appearance!

First of Class Withdrawn: 33028 (1963)
Last of Class Withdrawn: 33006/20/7 (1966)
Example Preserved: 33001

Above: Another view of No 33013, in final condition, with additional mud-hole washout plugs on the firebox side. The large sandboxes between the coupled wheels are well illuminated together with the leading sandbox, which was integral with the footstep and bufferbeam. The overall appearance of the Q1s remained the same throughout their careers. To No 33028 of the class fell the doubtful honour of being the first Bulleid engine (apart from the ill-fated 'Leader' class and the CIE 'Turf Burner' to be withdrawn from service, February 1963, due to a defective cylinder. This marked the commencement of the onslaught which was to see Bulleid steam vanish in such a dramatic manner over the next four years./*J. C. Haydon*

SECTION 3(a)

4–6–2 Class WC (BR power class 7P*)
Passenger Engines

Introduced: 1945
Total: 66†
'West Country'

* Originally 6P; later 7P5F.
† Total for 'West Country' class out of grand total of 110 Light Pacific's

Apparently undaunted by the prolonged teething troubles experienced with his first Pacific design, Bulleid pressed ahead with the design of a lightweight scaled-down version; intended for use on the many restricted secondary routes (apart from a few branch lines) which the SR owned, and over which the 'Merchant Navy' class were prohibited on account of weight.

In June 1945, just as Britain was celebrating the long hoped-for cessation of the war in Europe, and beginning to look to the future, the first Light Pacific was completed at Brighton Works and very appropriately turned out in full Malachite green livery, instead of the dead black of wartime. As the priority area for service was the West Country and the West of England main line, the Southern decided to call the new Pacifics the 'West Country' class. They were intended for both passenger and freight trains (the latter essentially vacuum-fitted) and they were generally similar in appearance to the 'Merchant Navy' class. Comparison with the

larger Pacifics showed that the chief dimensional differences were the cylinder bore, reduced by $1\frac{5}{8}$in to $16\frac{3}{8}$in; the piston stroke was the same, at 24in; the grate area was reduced to 38.25sq ft from $48\frac{1}{2}$sq ft; and the evaporative and superheating surfaces were

Top right: First of the class, No 21C101 *Exeter* in as-built condition, with full post-war livery of Malachite green with yellow lining and black trim. In effect the 'West Country' was a scaled-down, lightweight version of the 'Merchant Navy', with a reduced axle-load and restricted loading gauge, intended for use on the many secondary routes where the larger Pacifics were not allowed. The cab width was reduced to 8ft 6in (compared with 9ft for a 'Merchant Navy') and the locomotive weight was brought down to 86 tons, with a tender weighing $42\frac{1}{2}$tons and carrying 5tons of coal and 4500gal of water. The overall appearance closely followed that of the larger Pacifics, although for some reason difficult to define, they seemed the neater of the two Pacific designs. No 21C101 was officially named at Exeter station on 10 July 1945./*Author's Collection*

Below right: Royal special returning from Tattenham Corner on Derby Day 1946, entering Victoria (Eastern side) behind new Light Pacific No 21C132 (later named *Camelford)* with four-disc headcode and burnished buffers and drawgear. The driver has his head well out of the cab window, to enable him to see ahead of the engine on the curved approach to the bufferstops. A criticism of these engines, with their narrower cab and smoke deflectors, was their restricted forward visibility, although at this stage the smoke deflectors were very short and were later lengthened somewhat. /*P. Ransome-Wallis*

Below: The diagram illustrates the initial batch of 'West Country' Pacifics, as built.

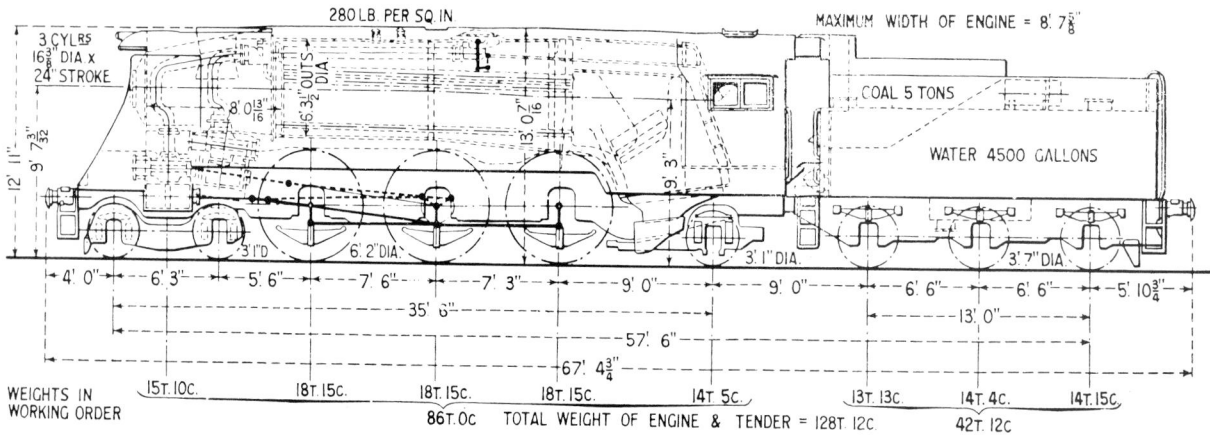

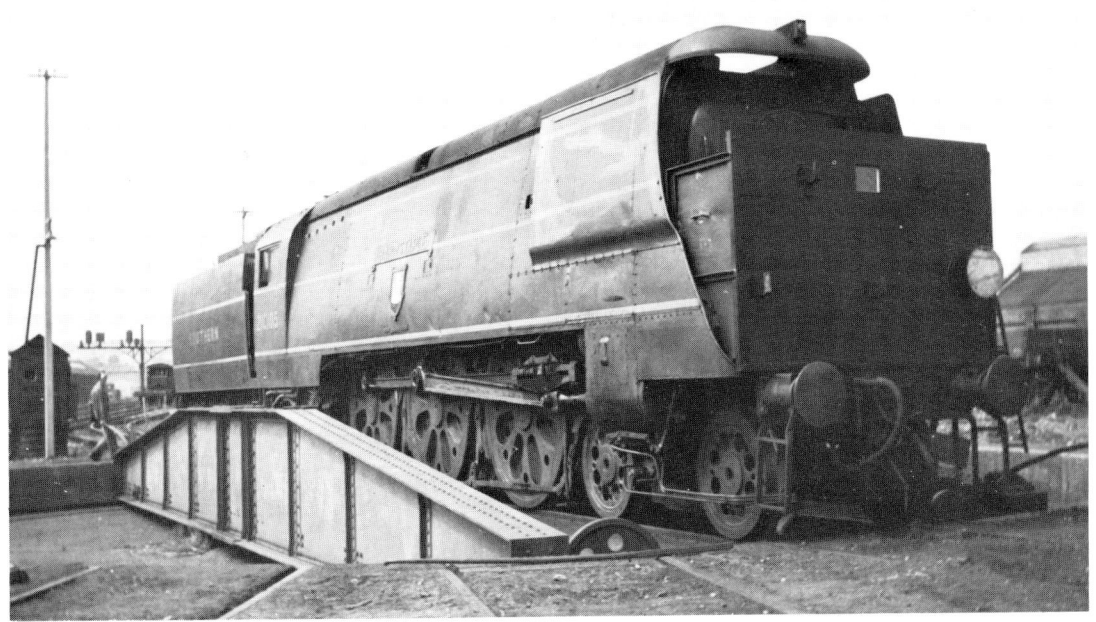

Above: A serious problem arose with the fracture of main frames on the Pacifics, with the main area of weakness being revealed at the front end, ahead of the cylinders. To allow study of the stresses and movement of the front end area, in relation to the main frames as a whole, two 'West Country' Pacifics were fitted with indicator shelters in 1946. These were Nos 21C105 *Barnstaple* and 21C139 *Boscastle*. The illustration depicts No 21C105 on the turntable at Brighton Works during the tests. Comparison with the illustration on page 49 reveals an intermediate stage in the length of the smoke deflector wingplates, which had already been lengthened since the locomotive was built. */H. M. Madgwick*

Left: The frontal aspect of the lightweight Pacifics was generally similar to the solution arrived at for the 'Merchant Navy' locomotives and comparison with the illustrations on pages 32 and 35 will show the minor detail differences which existed between the final batch of 10 'Merchant Navy' class and the initial Light Pacifics, in this respect. No 21C101 *Exeter* was built at Brighton, but the circular smokebox door ownership plate did not carry this information – only the year of building: 1945. */Author's Collection*

respectively 329 and 277sq ft less, at 2122 sq ft and 545sq ft. Boiler pressure was the same, at 280lb psi. The boiler barrel length was reduced by only $1\frac{1}{2}$in, but the diameter at the front was reduced to 5ft 6in, compared to 5ft $9\frac{3}{4}$in.

The shorter firebox allowed a reduction of 1ft for the distance between the trailing truck and the rear coupled axle (9ft) and the overall wheelbase was reduced to 35ft 6in, compared to 36ft 9in for a 'Merchant Navy'. The locomotive weight was effectively reduced from $94\frac{3}{4}$tons to 86tons. The weight on each coupled axle was 18tons 15cwt (against the 21tons of the 'Merchant Navy'), the bogie carried 15tons 10cwt and the trailing axle was loaded to 14tons 5cwt. The tender fitted had a water capacity of 4500gal and 5tons of coal, and weighed $42\frac{1}{2}$tons in working order, compared to $47\frac{3}{4}$tons for the larger engines. The tractive effort, at 85per cent of working pressure, was 31 000lb against the 37 500lb of the larger engine. In fact, the Maunsell 'Lord Nelson' was theoretically more powerful, with a tractive effort of 33 510lb, but with their larger boilers the Light Pacifics proved themselves superior in sustained haulage capacity and turn of speed, although heavier on coal.

No less than 70 of the new class were ordered in one go and there seems to have been

Above: No 21C138, as yet un-named (later *Lynton)*, is seen passing Sydenham Hill with an up morning Continental boat train for Victoria. The very narrow forward cab window is evident in this view; a distinct improvement was later made, with the introduction of the wedge shape (see next illustration), and in the final 40 engines the cab was 9ft wide instead of 8ft 6in. In August 1946 the Government announced a plan for the conversion of over one thousand steam locomotives, of all four railways, to burn oil instead of coal. The Southern included 20 'West Country' Pacifics in their list of chosen engines. First of the class to be converted was No 21C119 *Bideford*, in July 1947, followed by No 21C136 *Westward Ho!*, which had more sophisticated and successful equipment. The Government then proceeded to abandon the project, and both engines were soon restored to coal burning. */E. R. Wethersett*

none of the hesitation which surrounded the larger Pacifics in their early days. The 'West Country' class soon made an impression on services west of Exeter, at last relieving the hard-working 2–6–0s of Maunsell's U and N classes which had soldiered on with the heavier loads of wartime. In order to allow the new engines the widest possible route availability Bulleid restricted the cab width to 8ft 6in, compared to 9ft, so that they could be used on the Tonbridge and Hastings route, although this never materialised.

Most of the features that Bulleid had introduced with the 'Merchant Navy' class were perpetuated in the lightweight engines, including the air-smoothed casing, the patent valve gear, the BFB wheel centres, the clasp brakes, the thermic syphons and the oil bath enclosing the motion. Welding was again widely used in the construction of the engine and tender, and was an important factor in weight saving. Like the 'Merchant Navy' class,

the Light Pacifics were fitted with turbo-generators providing current for the headcode lamps on engine and tender, the cab and gauge lamps and the illumination of details for examination purposes.

As mentioned above, the new engines were never used over the restricted Tonbridge-Hastings route, so the reduced width of the cab was not necessary. Some criticism was forthcoming on the limited forward visibility which resulted, and various experiments with smoke deflector design took place, as can be seen in the accompanying illustrations. Finally, the flat-fronted cab was altered to a wedge shape which enabled a larger window to be fitted. Commencing with Battle of Britain class No 21C164 (see page 56) this modification was applied as the engines were built, and from No 21C171 onwards the cab width was increased to 9ft.

Confusion sometimes arises from the Southern Railway's decision to label the

Above: Immediately apparent is the extension of the smoke deflector wingplates to roughly twice their original length, on No 34005 *Barnstaple*, seen here entering St. Pancras station during the 1948 Locomotive Exchange Trials, with a train from Manchester. The Bulleid notation, 21C105, has been replaced by the new BR numbering, 34005, but the circular smokebox ownership plate is retained. The engine is attached to an LMS Stanier water-scoop tender (painted black) for use during the trials. Nos 34004/5/6 were selected to represent the class in the Exchanges, all with LMS tenders. The engines put up some really sparkling performances, particularly in Scotland, where No 34004 worked on the Perth-Inverness section, fitted with tablet apparatus. The cab has been rebuilt with a wedge shape at the front, to improve forward visibility./*C. C. B. Herbert*

Below: During the period of experimentation with locomotive liveries in 1948, when the newly created Railway Executive was trying to finalise new standard liveries for the nationalised system, a number of locomotives on each Region were selected for public display in proposed colours. The engines were rostered to stock in various livery alternatives and the travelling public was asked to express their preferences. One of the colours which was thankfully not adopted was a particularly bright apple green, with red, yellow and grey lining. No 34011 *Tavistock* is seen here in this rather unattractive garb (see also page 59), with the added splash of colour provided by the red-and-yellow 'Devon Belle' nameboards. Smoke deflector wing plates are extended to intermediate (and finalised) length. Photographed at Exmouth Junction, 28 July 1949./*Collection: N. E. Preedy*

Right: In May 1949, 'Battle of Britain' Pacific No 34059 *Sir Archibald Sinclair* was loaned to the Great Eastern section of the Eastern Region, where it worked to Norwich and Parkeston Quay. In 1951 three Light Pacifics were on loan to Stratford shed, and two ER 'Britannia' Pacifics (Nos 70009/14) were on loan to the Southern, later followed by No 70004 which was exibited at the Festival of Britain. The Bulleid engines were not popular with the GE crews and soon returned home. No 34039 *Boscastle* is seen here at Ipswich, with a train of LMR stock on 1 September 1951. /*H. C. Casserley*

engines as two different classes, as they were in actuality all the same. However, the publicity which this created was certainly worthwhile and I have followed their example by describing the 'Battle of Britain' engines in a separate sub-section, on pages 56-65. The first of the 'Battle of Britain' series was No 21C149, although it ran for some time without nameplates and was at first described as a 'West Country' — just to add to the confusion.

Some truly brilliant performances, by keen enginemen made the Light Pacific design one of the stars of the 1948 Locomotive Exchanges (in which three 'West Country' engines participated, Nos 34004/5/6, ex-Nos 21C104/5/6) although the published results of the tests later revealed a heavy coal consumption. The lightweight Pacifics were to display all the

Right: Commencing with No 34091 a further series of 'West Country' Pacifics appeared, up to No 34108. These never carried Malachite green livery, appearing instead in the standard dark BR Brunswick green, with orange and black lining and lion and wheel emblem, as seen here on No 34103 *Calstock,* working the 'Golden Arrow' Pullman in fine style through the chalk cuttings of the North Kent downs. These had tenders of 5500gal capacity, weighing 47.25tons. These engines had a 9ft-wide cab, and wedge-shape front cab windows from new./*F. R. Hebron*

Top: Although in BR Brunswick green livery and with the front-end casing removed ahead of the cylinders, No 34028 *Eddystone* still carried the original cab when this photograph was taken. No 34028 was selected for rebuilding by BR and of course received a wider 9ft cab with wedge-shape windows in the process; it reappeared in the rebuilt state in March 1958, (see section 7, page 90, for details of the rebuilt Light Pacifics.)/*J. Davenport*

Above: Before the BR rebuilding scheme commenced, there was always a degree of fascination in viewing a Bulleid Pacific in the partially undressed state which workshop overhaul produced. It was a reminder of the orthodox appearance of the 'works' beneath the air-smoothed shroud, and an indication of the inconvenience caused to maintenance staff. A bogie with BFB wheels is in the foreground; the locomotive is No 34038 *Lynton*, photographed in July 1953./*R. H. Clark*

same weaknesses as their larger brethren as time went on, and eventually they were selected for rebuilding along very similar lines, as described in Section 7 on pages 90-97. But it would be less than justice to dismiss these remarkable engines in such a manner. If they had their failings, they also had many fine qualities, including a wonderful boiler of incredible steaming capacity. Their reduced weight allowed them to roam far and wide over the Southern system, and they were the first engines larger than the N class 2–6–0s, allowed to travel over the Meldon Viaduct. During the Locomotive Exchanges they broke new ground for the Pacific wheel arrangement over the Highland line from Perth to Inverness and the Midland line from St Pancras to Manchester.

Construction of the Bulleid Light Pacifics was to continue after he had retired from the nationalised Southern Region in September 1949, and a total of 110 locomotives of the 'West Country' and 'Battle of Britain' classes was completed when 'Battle of Britain' No. 34110 *66 Squadron* appeared from Brighton in January 1951. Some speculation had surrounded this final engine of the class, which was delayed in construction for some months (No 34109 had been completed in May 1950) and rumour had it that the engine would not have Bulleid's valve gear. Nonetheless, it emerged in due course in full Bulleid form, in the very same month that the first BR standard two-cylinder Pacific No. 70000 *Britannia* appeared from Crewe. The tide was turning against the Bulleid engines and some of them had very short careers before rebuilding, as described in Section 7, after which they had a

Above: Comparison with the picture of No 34028 opposite shows some further modifications that were made to the 'West Country' locomotives in BR days. The cab has the improved wedge-shape front windows, and the tender has been cut down. The air-smoothed casing ahead of the cylinders has been removed and the locomotive carries BR AWS equipment on the front end. This was one of the 50 Light Pacifics which were never rebuilt by BR, and is seen here in the final form in which it ran. No. 34041 *Wilton* was photographed in ex-works condition at Eastleigh on 10 October 1963. The livery of locomotive and tender no longer matched, and the smooth lines of Bulleid's original conception were completely disrupted by the various modifications that had been made./*G. Wheeler*

family resemblance to the standard BR Pacifics. So late in the day was this programme of rebuilding undertaken that financial justification did not exist for the rebuilding of all 110 locomotives, and 50 were left to run out their days in original Bulleid form. No 34104 was the last to be rebuilt, in May 1961.

The 'West Country' class engines were built as follows:

Nos 21C101-21C148	Brighton	1945/6
Nos 34091-34109	Brighton	1949/50
	Eastleigh*	

Nos 21C101-21C148 were renumbered 34001-34048 respectively in 1948, by British Railways.

Nos 34095/7/9/101/2/4 built at Eastleigh

53

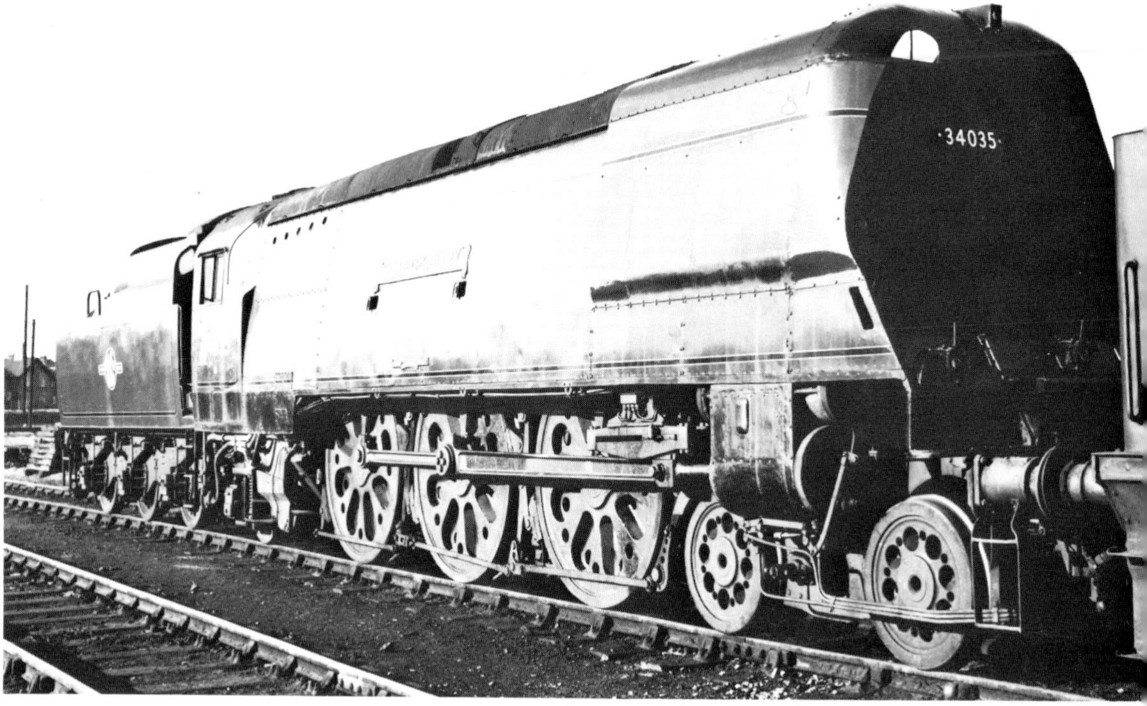

Above: Light work for a Light Pacific. 'West Country' No 34043 *Combe Martin* is seen here leaving Midford with the 4.35 pm Bath-Templecombe local train. Note the battery box for BR AWS above the bufferbeam. Trials with a 'Battle of Britain', No 34109 *Sir Trafford Leigh Mallory* (of Bournemouth shed), in 1951 led to the use of some Light Pacifics over the difficult Somerset & Dorset route, for which they were fitted with automatic tablet exchanging apparatus /*Derek Cross*

Left: A number of attempts were made to improve the draughting and exhaust dispersal of the Light Pacifics over a period of years. No 21C162 was modified in 1947, with curved deflector plates which apparently did not produce results. Another attempt is seen here, on No 34035 *Shaftesbury*, which had the cowling carried down to join the smoke deflectors (similar to the wartime experiments on No 21C10, see page 24.) The engine is seen in this modified form, at Eastleigh on 12 April 1960, with BR AWS equipment on the front end. Another experiment was made on 'Battle of Britain' No 34049, as illustrated on page 62./*L. Elsey*

Below: Coaling operations at Bournemouth Motive Power Depot, with the aid of a mechanical shovel, 7 June 1965. The rebuilt tender of No 34103 *Calstock* is well illustrated, with the electric lighting and two welded tubular ladders on the rear. Although 25kv catenary electrification warning signs are also carried, the engines seldom found themselves in such a location./*P. L. Simpson*

Modifications were made to the tender by BR, by removing the raves to allow the water to column bag to swing across the back, without obstruction, when filling the tank: No 34043 was the first to receive a modified tender, in June 1952. In common with the 'Merchant Navy' Pacifics the boiler pressure of all the Light Pacifics was reduced from 280lb to 250lb psi over a period of some two years from 1954-6. Rebuilding commenced in the summer of 1957 with No 34005 *Barnstaple*.

†*First of West Country Class Withdrawn (Unrebuilt):* 34035, 34043 (1963)
Last of West Country Class Withdrawn (Unrebuilt): 34023, 34102 (1967)
Example Preserved* (Unrebuilt): 34023.

*At the time of writing it was possible that a further example of the class in their original form might still be saved from the scrapyard, this was No 34105.
†*Withdrawal dates and examples preserved for the rebuilt engines are given on page 97.*

4–6–2 Class BB (BR power class 7P*)
Passenger Engines
Introduced: 1946
Total: 44†
'Battle of Britain'

Originally 6P, later given as 7P5F.

†*Total for Battle of Britain class, out of grand total of 110 Light Pacifics*

The decision to name some of the Light Pacifics in honour of the Battle of Britain was an excellent piece of public relations work, coming so soon after the restoration of peacetime working on the Southern Railway, and it undoubtedly helped to bring Bulleid's engines to the attention of the public at large. They were identical to the 'West Country' class, but tended to be thought of as a separate entity, and I have therefore segregated them accordingly.

The first naming ceremonies were suitably near the anniversary date of the Battle of Britain, in September 1947, by which time a number had run for some months without nameplates, and a particularly nice gesture was the choice of name for No. 34090 (last of a batch of 20 built in 1948/9,) which became *Sir Eustace Missenden Southern Railway,* and received full SR Malachite green livery.

It was a member of the 'Battle of Britain' class which was involved in the Lewisham disaster of 4 December 1957, at the Nunhead Flyover between Lewisham St. John's and Park

Right: Freak numbering for *Biggin Hill* in the early months of nationalisation; the Bulleid notation 21C157 has had the prefix "S" added to denote Southern Region (on the cabside,) whilst the smokebox carries neither the Bulleid circular brass ownership plate nor the later BR standard smokebox numberplate. The casing ahead of the right-hand cylinder appears to have taken a knock; this portion was later removed from the engines./*E. R. Wethersett*

Below right: Positively sparkling, in ex-works condition new 'Battle of Britain' Pacific No 21C168 *Kenley,* photographed at Brighton on 7 November 1947, in full post-war Malachite green livery with yellow lining and black trim to the lower portions of engine and tender sides./*British Rail SR*

Below: 'Battle of Britain' Pacific No 21C164 (later named *Fighter Command)* had the honour of being the 1000th locomotive built at Brighton Works. A special ceremony was held in the works yard on 9 June 1947 to commemorate the event. Coupled to the Pacific was the ex-LBSCR Stroudley 'Terrier' 0–6–0T No 82 *Boxhill,* which was restored to the famous Stroudley livery of 'improved engine green'. The two locomotives provided a truly remarkable contrast in aesthetic form. The Bulleid engine is seen here with the original cab design, but it actually entered traffic with the modified cab, being the first locomotive to receive this./*P. F. Winding*

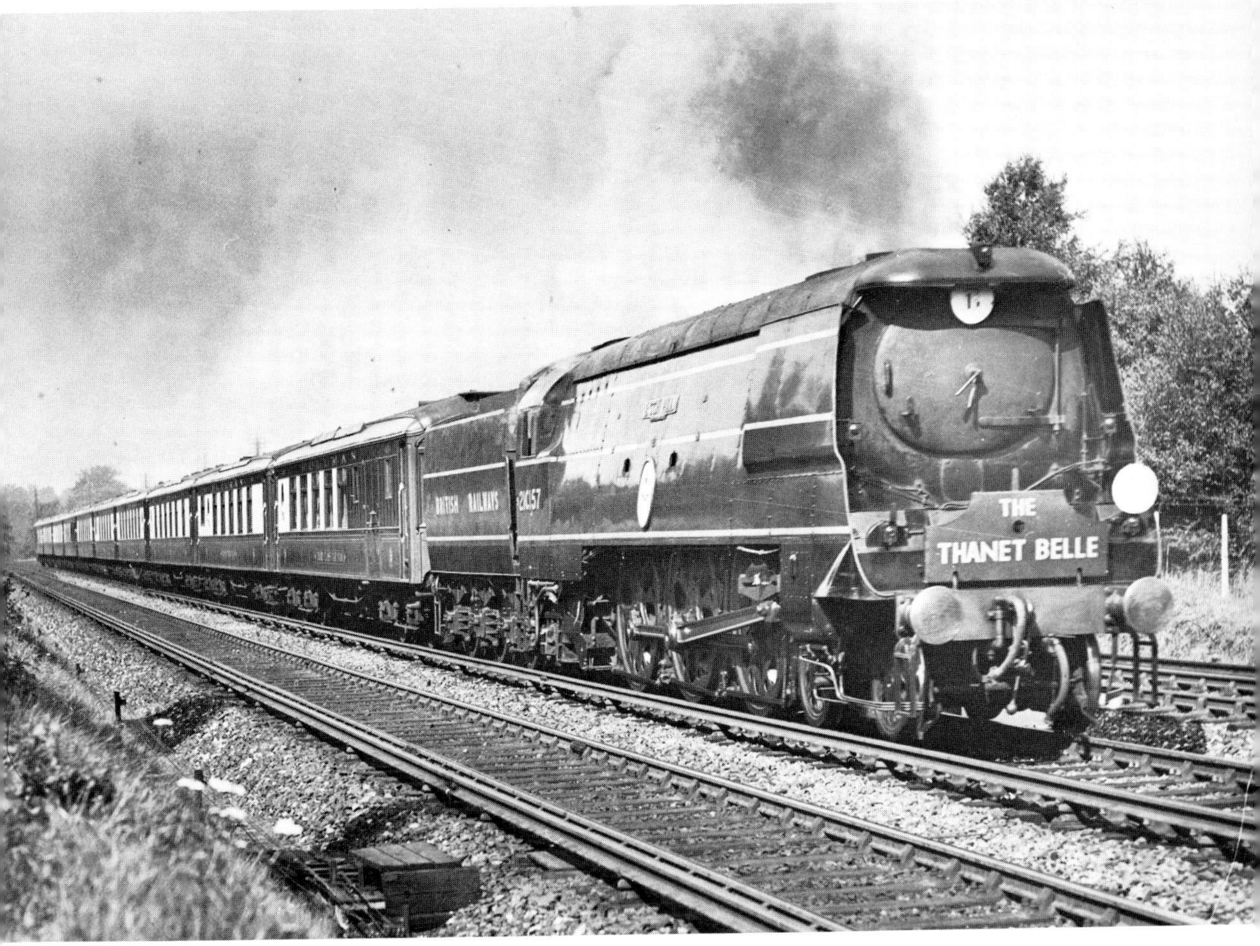
THE
THANET BELLE
BRITISH RAILWAYS
21C157

KENLEY
21C168
SOUTHERN
21C168

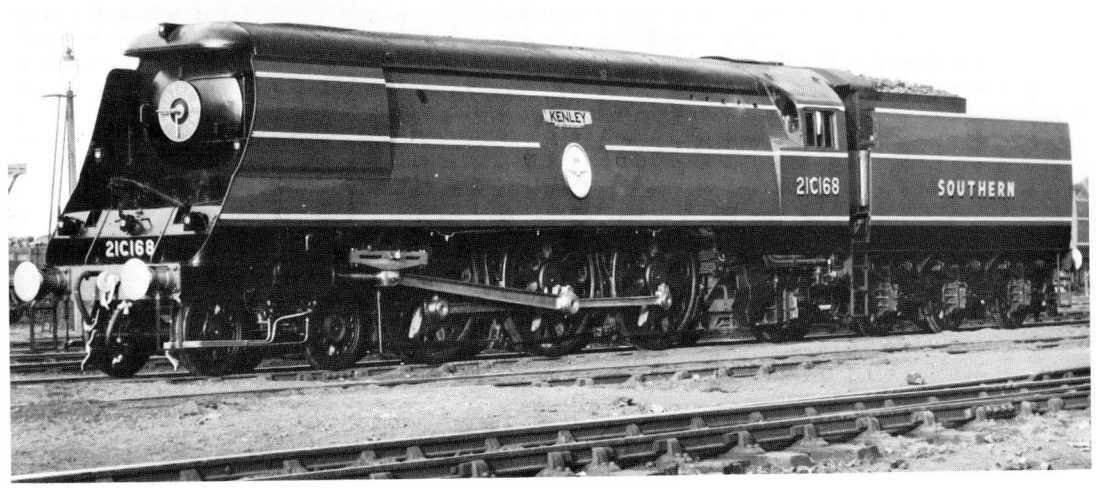

Bridge. The locomotive, No 34066 *Spitfire*, was working the 4.56pm down Cannon Street to Ramsgate train when it collided in foggy weather with the rear of the 5.18pm electric train from Charing Cross to Hayes. The crash also involved a train passing over the flyover and 90 people died in the ghastly pile-up. The engine was repaired and later returned to traffic.

The 'Battle of Britain' class engines were built as follows:

Nos 21C149-21C170	Brighton	1946/7
Nos 34071-34090	Brighton	1948/9
Nos 34109-34110	Brighton	1950/1

Nos 21C149-21C170 were renumbered 34049-34070 respectively, by BR in 1948.

No doubt because they were newer than the 'West Country' engines (except for Nos. 34091-34108) the 'Battle of Britain' engines were less affected by the BR rebuilding programme. Only 17 engines out of a total of 44 were rebuilt, compared with 43 'West Country' class out of a total of 66.

Right: Experimental livery of apple green with red, cream and grey lining and Gill sans lettering and numerals, applied to No 34086 (later named *219 Squadron*) at Brighton works, as part of an attempt to decide the new locomotive liveries for the nationalised system in 1948 (see also page 50.) The thin lining was not as effective as Bulleid's original scheme./*Lens of Sutton*

Below: Brand-new Pacific No 34076 (later named *41 Squadron*) in Bulleid livery but carrying BR numbering and lettering, painted in Southern style. From No 34071 onwards the Bulleid notation was never applied, as the locomotives were delivered after nationalisation. These engines were built new with the wider 9ft cab and had sweptback, wedge-shaped cab-front windows, which were later applied to the earlier batch on rebuilding (see pages 91-92.)/*Ian Allan Library*

Above: Although not constructed until February 1949, 'Battle of Britain' Pacific No 34090 was finished in full Southern Railway livery of Malachite green, with yellow lining and black trim; however, the new BR emblem appeared on the tender. The reason behind this was the choice of name for the locomotive – *Sir* *Eustace Missenden, Southern Railway* – a tribute to the last Chairman of the system prior to nationalisation. Illustrated is the tender of No 34090 in as-built condition. Tender capacity of Nos 34071-90 was 5500 gal. /*British Rail SR*

†*First of 'Battle of Britain' Class Withdrawn (Unrebuilt):* 34055 (1963).
Last of 'Battle of Britain' Class Withdrawn (Unrebuilt): 34057 (1967)
**Example Preserved (Unrebuilt):* 34051

*At the time of writing it was possible that further examples of the class in their original form might still be saved from the scrapyard. These were Nos 34081/92.
†Withdrawal dates and examples preserved for the rebuilt engines are given on page 97.

Left: Stewarts Lane could always be relied upon to turn out an immaculate locomotive for a special such as a royal train, or the visit of a foreign dignity. Witness the beautiful grooming of the front end of 'Battle of Britain' Pacific No 34088 *213 Squadron* when selected to work the royal train conveying the Emperor of Ethiopia on the occasion of his state visit, 14-16 October 1954. Comparison with the illustration on page 57 reveals only minor alteration to the front end since the original Light Pacifics had been introduced nine years earlier./*British Rail SR*

Above: A second view of No 34088 *213 Squadron* whilst specially groomed for the State visit of Haile Selassie, the Emperor of Ethiopia, taken as the locomotive hauled the Pullmans from Portsmouth to Victoria on 14 October 1954. Decorative headboard and white wheel tyres complete the splendid picture. /*Pursey C. Short*

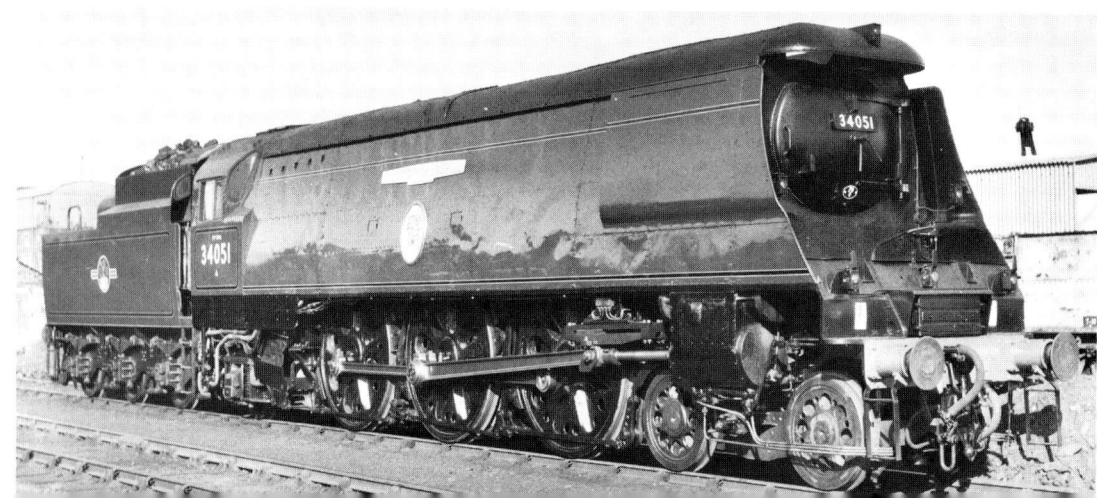

Top left: 'Battle of Britain' class 4–6–2 No 34055 *Fighter Pilot*, photographed at Salisbury shed on 6 June 1959 in BR dark green livery. The portion of casing ahead of the cylinders has been removed, but otherwise the engine is substantially in original condition, except for the modified cab windows./*P. H. Wells*

Centre left: The problems of smoke deflection and draughting remained unresolved until the BR rebuilding removed the air-smoothed casing entirely, greatly improving those members of the WC and BB lighweights which were so dealt with. Many experiments were tried on the Bulleid Pacifics, including complete removal of the smoke deflector wingplates, as seen here, on No 34049 *Anti-Aircraft Command,* photographed at Eastleigh on 19 February 1960. Note the handholds cut into the front end of the air-smoothed casing, and the continuation of the side sheets into the cowling ahead of the chimney./*L. Elsey*

Bottom left: The tenders of all the Light Pacifics were rebuilt in cut-down form, irrespective of whether the locomotive was selected for rebuilding or not. No 34051 *Winston Churchill* is seen here in ex-works condition at Eastleigh on 13 October 1963, carrying BR AWS equipment and 25kV warning signs on the front end. On 30 January 1965 this locomotive had the sad distinction of hauling the special funeral train conveying the body of Sir Winston Churchill, from Waterloo to Handborough./*G. Wheeler*

Below: Time took its toll on the air-smoothed outer casing of Bulleid's Pacifics, as is clearly seen in the raking light falling on No 34057 *Biggin Hill*, photographed in the shed yard at Nine Elms one February night./*V. C. K. Allen*

64

Above: Close-up of the characteristic narrow chimney of the Giesl Oblong Ejector, fitted to No 34064 in August 1962. Seven nozzles, with blower jets between them, were arranged in line to exhaust upwards to the narrow chimney, with a notable improvement in the draughting. A scheme to fit 20 or so more of the unmodified Light Pacifics was not pursued, as by this time expenditure on steam was not regarded with favour by BR management, although the performance of No 34064 after this modification was generally excellent. The main reason for the experiment was an attempt to reduce the sparkthrowing charactistic of the Bulleid engines, an unfortunate feature which was not appreciated by farmers and other lineside dwellers./*P. H. Groom)*

Left: Nearing Padstow with the 'Atlantic Coast Express' from Waterloo on 8 May 1964, 'Battle of Britain' No 34054 *Lord Beaverbrook* makes a pleasing picture and provides a useful comparison to the illustration above showing the wide diameter chimney of the Bulleid multiple-jet blastpipe./*S. C. Nash*

SECTION 4

0–6–6–OT 'Leader' class
(BR power class 5MT)
Mixed-Traffic Engines
Introduced: 1949
Total: 1*

Five were ordered and three were brought to an advanced stage of construction but only one entered trial service.

It was in the course of his presidential address to the Institute of Mechanical Engineers, in October 1946, that Bulleid first revealed to the public his new concept in tank engine design, stating that the first five of a class of 35 had been authorised. Some two years later, in the course of another address, this time to the British Association for the Advancement of Science, Oliver Bulleid released some advance information on the twelve-wheeled tank locomotive, to be known as the 'Leader' class, the first of which was nearing completion at Brighton Works. In the interim, the Southern Railway had been absorbed into the new nationalised system and Bulleid was designated the Chief Mechanical Engineer of the Southern Region of British Railways. There was much work, Bulleid said, for which tender engines were not necessary; to cover such duties – and indeed to meet practically all requirements – a tank engine was needed that would be able to work passenger and goods trains over all the system, with certain unimportant exceptions.

He listed the desirable features of this new tank engine as follows:

1 To be able to run over the majority of the company's lines.
2 To be capable of working all classes of trains up to 90mph.
3 To have its whole weight available for braking and the highest percentage thereof for adhesion.
4 To be equally suitable for running in both directions without turning, with unobstructed lookout.
5 To be ready for service at short notice.
6 To be almost continuously available.
7 To be suitable for complete "common use".
8 To run not less than 100 000 miles between general overhauls with little or no attention at the running sheds.
9 To cause minimum wear and tear to the track.
10 To use substantially less fuel and water per drawbar horsepower developed.

Below: 'Leader' class 0–6–6–OT, showing fireman's side. The boiler was offset to allow a corridor to run between the driving cab at the smokebox end and the fireman's compartment amidships.

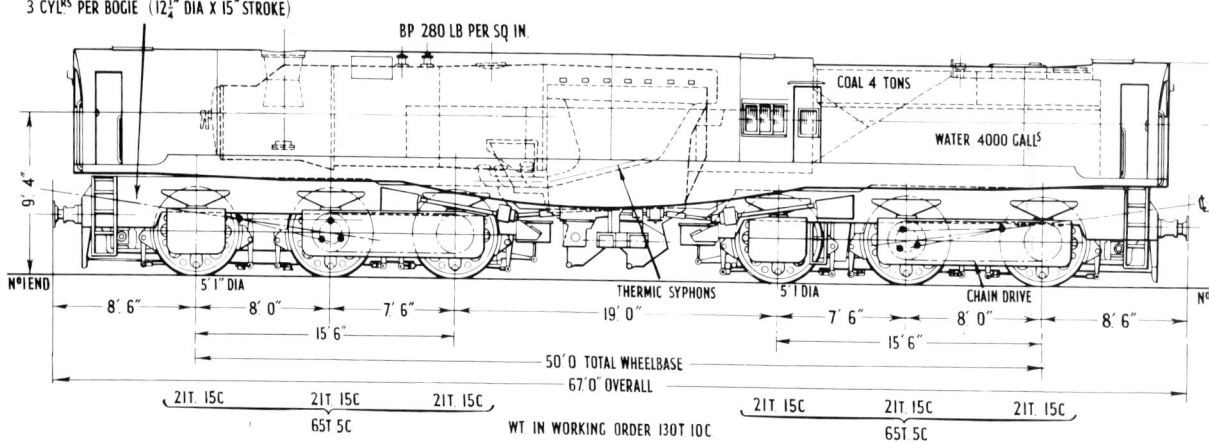

Various preliminary schemes preceded the final concept, including two tank engines based upon the Q1 goods engine, one an 0–6–2T, the other an 0–6–4T. There was even a proposal for a massive 4–6–4T, but by 1946 the double-ended 0–6–6–0T design was approved in principle. In retrospect it seems remarkable that Bulleid should have succeeded in convincing the Southern Railway management that such a large and indeed revolutionary steam locomotive was the answer to this traffic requirement – which was, in fact, initially supposed to replace a variety of elderly, modestly sized tank engines, such as the M7 0–4–4T. Of course, the one significant difference lay in the idea that a single locomotive could perform the whole range of duties, from branch line to main line, whereas in

Above: A new design of cylinder, which incorporated a sleeve valve, was produced by Bulleid for the 'Leader' class 0–6–6–0T, and in order to test this in service he chose ex-LBSCR Class H1 4–4–2 No 2039 *Hartland Point* as a partial guinea pig. This locomotive was modified in September 1947 with fabricated steel cylinders and sleeve valves operated by levers, chain-driven by sprockets attached at the centre of the driving axle. The front end was cut away and a plain chimney was provided, whilst the leading bogie was replaced by one from a Billinton D3 0–4–4T, with 3ft diameter wheels. Renumbered 32039 by British Railways, the adulterated Atlantic is seen here at Brighton Works in 1949, with 'Leader' class No 36001 in the background. Water consumption of No 32039 in modified form was prolific indeed./*P. F. Winding*

Above: Seen at Eastleigh in February 1951, in store prior to withdrawal from service. No 32039 *Hartland Point* was finally withdrawn a few weeks later. The modifications for the sleeve valve experiments certainly ruined the graceful lines of the Brighton Atlantic./*L. Elsey*

Above right: No 36001 at Lewes on 31 August, 1949 running bunker-first on a trial from Brighton to Crowborough. As usual, the fireman has both the door and window wide open in an attempt to keep a reasonable working temperature in the confined working space. The Locomen's representatives were not satisfied with the working conditions of the enginemen and only agreed to a volunteer crew operating No 36001, making it clear that they would require very considerable improvement in working conditions before the class entered service. Bulleid had envisaged oilfiring, which would have eased the problem, but there was also dissatisfaction at the remote location of the fireman's compartment, a feature which would have been more difficult to overcome without drastic redesign./*C. C. B. Herbert*

the past the two concepts were considered separately. To achieve this aim with steam traction would, he believed, require a type of locomotive quite unlike anything hitherto produced in Britain. Bulleid's own Light Pacifics had an admirable route availability, and a Class 7 power rating, but they did not answer to the more idealistic requirements he had set himself, in particular, the availability and freedom from routine shed maintenance. Nor did they have the maximum braking and adhesion factors that he envisaged.

The new 'Leader' class was intended to be a standard type, roughly equivalent in power to a Class 5 mixed-traffic engine, which together with the two Pacific classes could answer all needs other than those where electrification or dieselisation were viable propositions. Because so many new features were proposed, Bulleid sought and obtained authority to build five locomotives, rather than a single prototype, to be tried out in all classes of traffic over Southern metals.

I have already referred to the basic concept of the design, which was an 0–6–6–0T. The underframe was 65ft long and carried the

boiler; smokebox, bunker for 4tons of coal and tank for 4000gal of water, a driving cab at each end and a fireman's cab between the boiler and the bunker. All this was enclosed within an overall casing of rather angular aspect which had no pretentions towards either air-smoothing or streamlining.

The conventional boiler, which had a pressure of 280lb psi, was of modified design in so far as the side and back water spaces of the firebox were replaced by plain sheet steel lined with refractory material; four thermic syphons joined the crown of the firebox to the underside of the barrel. The idea was to avoid the maintenance associated with stayed firebox water spaces. In service this proved a troublesome feature, providing an overheated area which – apart from anything else – made the fireman's job intolerable.

The idea of providing a true mixed-traffic engine depended very much upon keeping the weight down, without sacrificing adhesion and brake power. The calculated tractive effort, at 85per cent of working pressure, was 26350lb, roughly equivalent to that of a conventional BR Class 5 locomotive. To meet requirement No. 1

on the list weight had to be kept down to $112\frac{1}{2}$tons in full working order (an axleload of $19\frac{3}{4}$tons.) In retrospect it seems odd that Bulleid should have attempted this with such a large locomotive when he already had a Class 7 Pacific (the 'West Country'/'Battle of Britain') which was light enough to work over most secondary routes. Only the more obscure branch lines were barred to the Light Pacifics, and these were worked by a variety of vintage tank engines of modest size and power. A problem which would have prevented the 'Leader' class (at least in its prototype form), from taking over these branch line duties was that it was proved to be far in excess of the heaviest permitted axle-load, whilst the power Class 5 meant that it would have a difficult task matching up to the excellent performances of the Light Pacifics when working over main lines.

The 'Leader' had Bulleid-Walschaerts valve gear operating sleeve valves with rotatory motion to equalise wear (as in internal combustion engine practice) with three fabricated steel cylinders per bogie. Cylinder bore was $12\frac{1}{4}$in and the stroke was 15in; the wheel diameter was 5ft 1in. The centre axle was a three-throw crank and there was a chain sprocket at each end, outside the wheels. The outer and inner axles were plain, each having a sprocket at opposite ends, and chains replaced conventional coupling rods – providing an unsymmetrical drive from the centre axle, a feature which later proved a cause of crank axle failures. The bogies had all their working parts enclosed in oil baths and were designed in such a way that they could be removed and interchanged, much in the manner adopted for electric traction.

The dawn of nationalisation saw work well in hand on the design, but Bulleid realised he was now involved in a race against time, because the new regime favoured more simplistic forms of steam locomotive development. No 36001 was completed at Brighton in June 1949 and commenced trial runs on 22 June. Teething troubles were plentiful and really only to be expected, but Bulleid was now 68 years old, and he left the Southern, and his protégé, to take up the post of Consulting Engineer to the CIE in the autumn. The new locomotive was now in the hands of BR, and so troublesome was it proving to be that an order was given on 19 November 1949 to stop work on the next four locomotives in Brighton erecting shop. At this time No

Below: Only the pioneer locomotive, No 36001, ever ran in steam, but never in revenue-earning service, being confined to trial runs, either light engine or hauling empty stock. The livery was shop grey with red and black lining and Gill Sans lettering. The pale patch of paintwork in the centre of the bodyside obliterated the BR lion and wheel emblem, with number below, which the locomotive briefly displayed when new. Steam can be seen issuing from the turbogenerator for the electric lighting, located between the first and second axles./*S. C. Nash*

Below right: Project abandoned. Uncompleted locomotive No 36003 had been towed to Bognor Regis Motive Power Depot for storage, pending dismantling; previously it had been stored at New Cross Gate. The partial exposure of the leading bogie shows the arrangement of the springs for the three BFB wheels and the sprockets for the chain-drive. The smokebox end of the boiler is visible. Photographed on 10 April, 1950 with the steam from 'Battle of Britain' 4–6–2 No 34069 *Hawkinge* standing on the adjacent track. The order to cease work on the construction of Nos. 36002-5 was given on 19 November, 1949, with No 36002 only two days from completion and No 36003 partially erected (as seen). Tests with No 36001 continued for a further year, with the locomotive transferred to Eastleigh works./*S. C. Nash*

36002 was just two days from completion and No 36003 was reasonably advanced.

Trials with No 36001 continued, but by June 1950 the locomotive had proved so far from serviceable that a last chance was given, with its transfer to Eastleigh where, it was hoped, the staff would have more success with it. A testing crew from York was sent, together with the ex-North Eastern Railway dynamometer car, for a series of trial runs which it was planned No 36001 should to work over the South Western main line between Eastleigh and Woking. For comparative purposes, the locomotive would haul a train of empty stock for a fortnight, with a Maunsell U class 2–6–0 working the same load the following fortnight.

A principal objection to the design was the inadequate and unbearably hot accommodation provided for the fireman, who was forced to wear protective sacking over his legs. Oil-firing would have reduced the discomfort, but it would not have removed the other objection — namely that he was in solitary confinement, out of immediate contact with the driver in the event of an emergency. The trials were not a success; there was trouble with the firebox and the engine was steaming badly. The crank axles broke and were replaced by axles from No 36002, but these broke also.

Weighbridge readings revealed the excess weight plus a disparity of wheel weight between one side and the other. A solution was sought by placing ballast weights down the side corridor, but this of course increased the overall weight of the locomotive still further. It is believed to have been somewhere in the region of 130tons.

In November 1950 the order came to cease work on No 36001; all tests were to stop and the other four uncompleted engines were to be scrapped. The locomotive was left in the open at Eastleigh, before final dismantling took place in 1951.

The engines were built as follows:

No 36001	Brighton	1949
No 36002*	Brighton	1949
Nos 36003-36005**	Brighton	1949

*Withdrawn when virtually completed, November 1949.
**Withdrawn whilst in course of erection, November 1949 (Nos 36002/3 were stored at New Cross Gate in 1949)
Entire class condemned, November 1950.

Left: Close-up of the front end of 'Leader' No 36001, showing the three cylinders located between the bogie frames, also the extension hoses from cab to bufferbeam for the vacuum brake and steam heating. The centre window opened outwards; the whistle was located above the right-hand window. Photographed at Eastleigh works on 1 October 1950./*L. Elsey*

Above: 'Leader' class 0–6–6–0T No 36001 is seen being dismantled in Eastleigh works, following the BR decision to abandon the project, in 1951. The last trial run was on 2 November 1950, when the persistent teething troubles showed no signs of easing and the locomotive was condemned. Weighbridge readings had earlier revealed that the locomotive was far in excess of the permitted axle load and also had a disparity of weight between one side and the other, largely due to the offset boiler. As a result, the weight of No 36001 had been further increased by the insertion of cast iron ballast in the side corridor, in order to effect a balance. This interesting photograph reveals the side corridor (complete with ballast weights) with the smokebox end of the locomotive nearest the camera. The fireman's compartment is visible amidships, with the bunker and water tank beyond. Bulleid had intended that the bogies should be removable en bloc for overhaul or repair, in a similar manner to the power bogies of electric stock. A shortcoming of the design was the need to remove large portions of the outer body casing in order to reach the boiler, etc, during examination or repair. Even the routine maintenance procedures for a steam locomotive — boiler washout, smokebox cleaning, and so on — were made difficult by the outer superstructure./*S. C. Townroe*

SECTION 5

0–6–6–OT
Mixed-Traffic Engine
Introduced: 1957
Total: 1
'Turf Burner'
Córas Iompair Eireann (CIE)

In a country which had to import almost all of its coal for steam traction, the existence of vast amounts of fuel in the form of peat, or turf, quickly attracted Bulleid to the idea of producing a locomotive design which could burn the native fuel. The disadvantages of turf were already well known to CIE, as various experiments had been made in the past. In particular it had a lower calorific value than coal and a greater quantity was required to produce the same heat output – roughly four times the volume in fact. Thus a greater quantity of ash resulted and the locomotive had to haul a tender of considerably larger capacity if enough fuel was to be carried. The second World War had seen a fuel famine on Eire's railways and despite the known problems turf was used, in the form of briquettes, as well as other lower grade fuels, down to anthracite dust. Even after the war the country was hit by a severe coal shortage (in 1947) and this time CIE used oil-burning apparatus to keep its steam locomotives in limited service. Of course, oil was also an imported fuel and there was no guarantee that similar shortages would not arise (as indeed they did) in the future. If a really successful turf-burning design could be pro-

duced, the fuel problems of CIE, in cases of national shortage, would be considerably reduced and this would allow them to operate a more adequate service. Even the final decision to dieselise the CIE motive power fleet did not deter Bulleid from his objective, as the 'Turf Burner' would be a standby for oil shortages, as well as being suitable power for the seasonal sugar-beet traffic – but that is to run ahead of the evolving story.

When O. V. S. Bulleid left the Southern Region of British Railways to take up his post with the CIE, he went straight to a railway which still operated a fleet of steam locomotives of high average age and of very mixed parentage. The CIE Board had rejected the idea of electrification because of the low density of the population, but had initiated limited use of diesel-electric traction, in the form of five shunting engines and two larger mixed-traffic locomotives. When Bulleid first outlined his ideas for future CIE traction he remained in favour of steam, using imported coal, rather than diesels using imported oil. The ideal – a turf burning steam locomotive – was already in his mind, but only in vague outline. For the moment he thought that a considerable reduction in the aged fleet of steam locomotives was essential; a new standard mixed-traffic design (probably a medium-powered 0–6–0 tank engine) should take their place.

By 1951 it was becoming clear that Bulleid's desire to retain steam was not meeting with the approval of the Government partly due to the ever-increasing cost of imported coal. The CIE Board again considered a switch to diesel traction, although Bulleid was by now able to

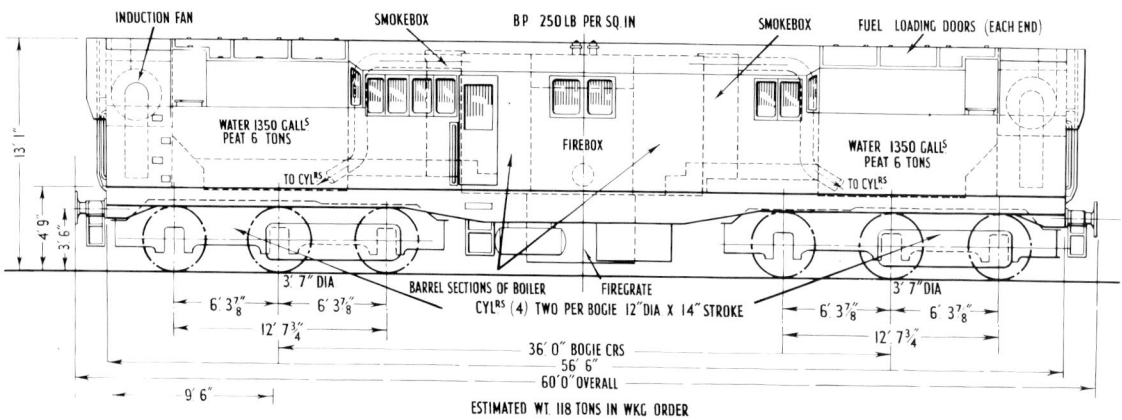

announce that some progress was being made with experiments with turf as a fuel. Diesel traction was, however, introduced in the form of railcars the same year, and by 1953 the CIE was committed to a programme of dieselisation. As already mentioned, Bulleid was not deterred by this, and in fact he gained authority to build fifty new steam locomotives, burning either turf or oil to supplement the new diesel fleet in periods of peak traffic.

The beginnings of the 'Turf Burner' project are traceable to about 1950. One early proposal was for a compression ignition engine, and there were also thoughts of using pulverised turf. Just as he had done when working on the 'Leader' design, Bulleid selected an existing locomotive to act as a guinea-pig. This was a 1907 Coey inside-cylinder 2–6–0, No 356. A new tender, using parts of an existing ex-Midland Great Western tender was provided, with greater fuel capacity and mounted upon lengthened frames. Behind the tender was coupled a four-wheel wagon, upon which was mounted a diesel-powered blower,

Above: Once again, as with the 'Leader', Bulleid selected an existing locomotive to act as a guinea-pig for his new ideas, this time an inside-cylinder 2–6–0, No 356. Conversion involved the fitting of a pair of preheating boilers alongside the existing boiler (one each side) and the provision of a mechanical stoker. A Franco-Crosti scheme was considered for this locomotive at one stage. The tender was rebuilt from an existing ex-MGWR tender. The chimney on the smokebox was provided for lighting-up purposes only; the real chimney was at the rear of the tender. The livery was aluminium and the tender was inscribed "CIE Experimental Turf Burning Locomotive"./T. K. Widd

Left: The locomotive is shown in final form, with smoke deflectors added.

Left: Running light engine, on trial from Inchicore, No CCI had rather primitive smoke-deflectors added by the time this picture was taken. Judging by the way the exhaust is clearing the drivers' lookout, these were effective in service. They were later improved in shape, as shown in the following illustration. The large fuel hopper and the water tank were duplicated at each end of the locomotive. No electric lights were fitted, and the locomotive carried conventional oil lamp headcodes./*J. G. Click*

Above: Still in workshop grey livery, No CCI is seen here at the head of some very mixed empty rolling stock during a trial run, at Sallins on 5 September 1957. The engine is in as-built condition. Trouble was experienced with spark throwing, on one occasion setting light to the roof of one of the elderly wooden carriages of the test train. Speeds of up to 70 mph were achieved on these test runs and the locomotive was reported to run as smoothly as a carriage. The draught was provided by fans, driven by turbines, and these gave the engine the advantage of being able to restore steam pressure very quickly after being worked hard. Before being exhausted through two chimneys, one each end of the cabs, the hot gases of combustion were led past feed heaters./*J .G. Click*

Left: No CCI, the 'Turf Burner' in final form, with smoke-deflectors added to the ends and painted bright green with yellow 'dazzle' stripes, lining and lettering. The 'dazzle' effect was added because the locomotive was extremely silent when running, soon earning the nickname of 'the quiet one'. A chime whistle was fitted and frequently used to warn of the engine's approach. The photograph was taken in the works yard at Inchicore, on 3 June 1961, with the project shelved, although the engine survived intact until 1965. It only worked a total of some 2000 miles all told, and never entered revenue-earning service./*S. C. Nash*

which created a draught. The locomotive was fitted with a pair of preheating boilers, each side of the boiler proper, and the flue gases and exhaust steam were used to preheat the boiler feed water in both the preheaters and in the tender, before being allowed to pass into the atmosphere through a chimney at the rear of the tender. Between 1952 and 1954 a series of trials and modifications took place with No 356 including, latterly, a venture onto the main line which ended in total failure at Cork.

Valuable lessons were learned from the experimental engine, which in itself was not considered a success. Once again – as so often in Bulleid's career – the sands of time were running out, and once again his remarkable powers of persuasion won the day. As mentioned earlier he sought, and gained, authority to proceed with the turf burning project despite a CIE decision to dieselise. His ideas had by now taken more definite form, and the layout of his new engine was clearly influenced by his final design for the Southern – the highly controversial 'Leader' class – in so far as it was to be an 0–6–6–0 double bogie tank engine. The boiler was in fact proportioned for oil fuel, but was also suitable for turf at a more restricted power output. Two mechanical stokers fed the crushed turf from the two fuel hoppers to the firebox, where it was spread by steam jets. Draughting was provided by a fan at each end of the locomotive, with the exhaust gases being discharged through chimneys in front of each cab. At the base of both chimneys there was a spark-arresting device, intended to deflect sparks back into the firebox. The cabs themselves were arranged, one for each direction of travel, and had a door only on the left-hand side facing the direction of travel; the cabs were located between the fuel bunkers and the central boilers and firebox.

The bogies were self-contained units, as in the 'Leader' class, and each had a two-cylinder steam engine with enclosed crankshaft and oil bath lubrication. External coupling of the axles was by means of chains, totally enclosed. The bogie wheel diameter was 3ft 7in, compared to 5ft 1in for the 'Leader,' and the drawgear and buffers were conventionally placed at the ends of the massive underframe, and not upon the bogies, as featured in the 'Leader' design. Each bogie had two brake cylinders. In reality the 'Turf Burner' was a very different locomotive to the 'Leader', and it was also considerably smaller and less powerful. It was only 60ft long,

compared to 76ft and the tractive effort was 19 926lb compared to 26 300lb. The square boiler had 250lb psi pressure. The entire layout was different, with a centralised firebox and two outer ends which duplicated all essential items, whereas the 'Leader' had conformed more to a normal locomotive layout, except for the location of the cabs at each end.

The locomotive was numbered CCI, in true Bulleid style, and was steamed at Inchicore in August 1957, making its first movements in steam in the works yard. Once out on the main line it displayed a tendency to throw sparks, but ran with remarkable quietness, soon earning the nickname of "the quiet one". Line tests were certainly more satisfactory than had been the case with the 'Leader', and one suspects that Bulleid had been successful in ironing out a lot of the problems he had encountered with his first 0–6–6–0T design. But although he demonstrated a considerable measure of technical success with No CC1 he was never to see the design become accepted and multiplied; yet again time had run out. In May 1958 he retired from his post of Chief Mechanical Engineer of the CIE. The locomotive was never tried out as an oil-burner (as Bulleid had intended should happen once he had proved its suitability for turf burning) and it had never run in revenue-earning service. By this time the CIE diesel programme was well under way and the locomotive was quietly placed in a siding at Inchicore. There it remained, cold and neglected, until 1965, a sad end to the last steam locomotive design by O. V. S. Bulleid and the last steam locomotive design produced for Ireland. The plan to build fifty was quietly forgotten – the diesel had won the day.

The engine was built as follows:

No CC1   Inchicore   1957

Withdrawal: 1965
Nominal (Never placed in CIE stock.)

The BR Rebuilds

The decision to modify the Bulleid Pacifics was finally taken in 1955. Compared to their counterparts on other Regions they were not wholly efficient engines and were heavy on oil and coal. Design proposals for a comprehensive modification of the 'Merchant Navy' class began to take shape at Brighton in 1954. The entire class was subsequently rebuilt, together with all but 50 of the 'West Country' and 'Battle of Britain' engines between 1956-61. With the writing already on the wall for steam traction in Britain, the careers of these rebuilt Pacifics were tragically short. R. G. Jarvis was in charge of the design work at Brighton and is quoted as saying that the engines remained 90 per cent Bulleid, even if they had lost the features to which he was specially attached.

4–6–2 Class 8P
Express Passenger Engines
(BR rebuild of Bulleid MN class)

Introduced: 1956
Total: 30
Modified 'Merchant Navy'

In 1955 authority was given for the rebuilding of 15 out of the 30 'Merchant Navy' class Pacifics, together with 15 of the Light Pacifics. The 'Merchant Navy' was tackled first, and in the early weeks of 1956 Eastleigh released No 35018 *British India Line* in modified form. Visually there was a distinct family likeness to the Riddles BR standard engines, although the distinctive Bulleid wheels were retained. The whole air-smoothed casing was removed and boiler clothing of conventional type was used instead, allowing ease of access and maintenance. Large smoke-deflectors were fitted, and the multiple-jet chimney had a pleasing form in cast iron. The original boiler was retained, at the lower pressure of 250lb psi, but a new saddle-supported cylindrical smokebox was fitted, using the original door.

The firegrate had a manually-operated rocking section in two parts and there were modifications to the triple ashpan of the original engines. A new superheater header was fitted and outside steampipes fed the two outside cylinders. The mechanical lubricators for the cylinders and valve chests were relocated on the running plate, instead of their original position beneath the smokebox frontplate (where they had been vulnerable to fire ash when the smokebox was cleaned). A new

Below: Modified 'Merchant Navy' Pacific, as reconstructed at Eastleigh, 1956-59, with 6000gal tender.

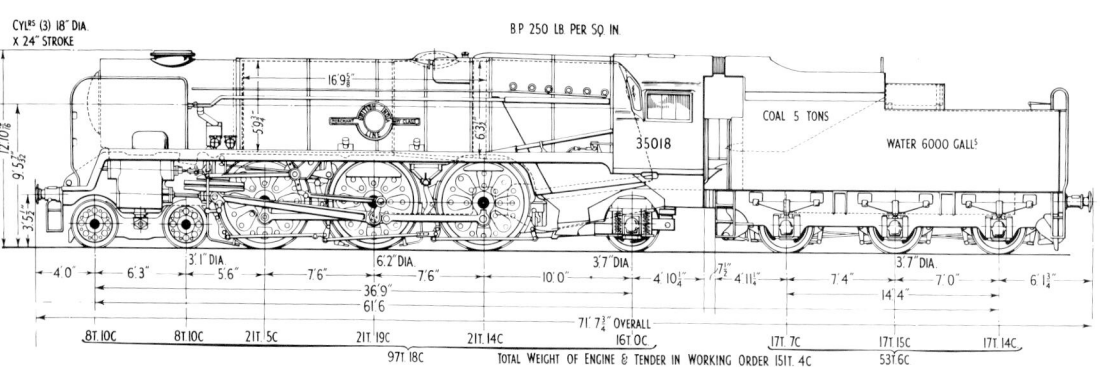

lubricator was provided for the slidebars and coupled axleboxes, replacing the multi-feed oil boxes in the cab. All the lubricators were driven from the expansion links of the outside valve motion.

The troublesome oil bath and chain-driven Bulleid valve gear was removed entirely, and three separate sets of Walschaerts valve motion were used; those for the outside cylinders were driven by return cranks placed on the driving crankpins, and by crosshead arms attached to the crossheads. The inside valve gear was driven by an eccentric mounted on the right-hand crank web of the driving axle. Maximum valve travel was $6\frac{3}{4}$ in for the outside

Above: The first 'Merchant Navy' to undergo modification was No 35018 *British India Line*, which appeared from Eastleigh early in 1956. A new saddle-supported cylindrical smokebox was provided, but the unique Bulleid smokebox door was retained. This view of No 35018 approaching completion suggests that they would have been exceedingly handsome engines minus the smoke deflectors. Three sets of Walschaerts valve gear replaced the unique and troublesome Bulleid chain-driven motion. The boiler was retained, at the lower pressure of 250lb psi introduced to the original engines by Jarvis in 1952. The layout of the sanding gear was revised for both the 'Merchant Navy' class and the Light Pacifics in their modified form, as explained in detail on page 95. */British Rail SR.*

valves and $6\frac{1}{4}$in for the inside valve. The steam reversing gear originally fitted was dispensed with and replaced by screw gear, with a cut-off indicator of the drum type. A single reversing shaft was fitted for the three valve gears, operated by slide blocks in the radius rod, a design developed on the LMS by Ivatt.

A new inside cylinder, with inside admission piston valves, and the steamchest offset to the right, formed part of the smokebox saddle together with a fabricated stretcher, which was attached to the main frames. Because the existing outside cylinders were retained, with their outside admission, the drive of the valve stem of the new piston valves was taken from the top pin of the combustion lever, instead of the second pin. In place of the usual valve-spindle crosshead, a suspension link supported this part of the gear. The original piston rod and crosshead were a single forging, and these were replaced by a separate crosshead with the normal cone and cotter attachment.

The cab structure remained unaltered, except that the lower portion of the curved side sheeting was cut away, partly to increase

Above: Pacific transformed. The first appearance of No 35018 *British India Line* at Waterloo was on 14 February 1956, when it was officially inspected. By the time this picture was taken, on Good Friday the same year, handrails had been added to the smoke deflectors. The engine is seen leaving on the 'Bournemouth Belle', with 'King Arthur' class 4-6-0 No 30457 *Sir Bedivere* alongside. /*F. Spencer Yeates*

Right: Close-up of the clever adaptation of the existing outside cylinders to take the Walschaerts valve gear. This also shows the location of mechanical lubricators and the new sandbox for the leading coupled wheels. The Bulleid clasp brakes are retained and balance weights have been added to the BFB coupled wheels. This official photograph was taken prior to the decision to fit handrails to the smoke deflectors /*British Rail SR.*

Top: The second engine to be modified was No 35020 *Bibby Line*, which emerged from Eastleigh in April 1956. For some weeks it ran with an unmodified 6000gal tender, as seen here, and this certainly gave a more massive appearance to the ensemble. No 35020 was selected for tests to prove the worth of the redesign, and undertook controlled road tests, as well as service tests, on the Waterloo-Salisbury-Exeter route. The engine was photographed at Eastleigh on 3 June 1956./*L. Elsey*

Above: Rebuilt 'Merchant Navy' 4-6-2 No 35027 *Port Line* stands in the sun at Eastleigh, attached to a modified 6000gal tender. The balance weight added to the centre coupled wheels is visible, also the speedometer on the rear coupled wheel. Photographed on 29 September 1961. Plain-section coupling rods were used for the rebuilt Pacifics./*G. W. Morrison*

accessibility and partly for appearance. A foothole was cut into the lower portion of the cab side and the original cab roof ventilator was replaced by a new one supported on links. Provision of the screw-operated reversing gear involved moving the driver's seat back slightly. The Ajax type firehole door was retained, but without the steam-operating gear, and a deflector plate was added to improve combustion.

Modification of the Pacifics tenders in fact preceded the engines by some three years or so, and was sufficiently under way for a number of locomotives to run with modified tenders in their original Bulleid form (see page 35.) The modification involved the removal of the side raves and the provision of compartments for the fireirons on either side of the bunker. The rear of the tender top was flat and a protective casing was placed over the vacuum reservoirs. All the existing MN tenders were so treated and a few of the smaller tenders received new 5250gal bodies on the original

frames; these were used on both the 'Merchant Navy' and the Light Pacifics. The weight in working order of a rebuilt 6000gal tender was given as 53.6tons, and the engine weighed 97.9tons in full working order in the rebuilt form.

The engines were rebuilt as follows:

Above: Seen in positively beautiful ex-works condition, at Eastleigh on 12 March 1964 is No 35029 *Ellerman Lines*, attached to a rebuilt 5000gal tender off the original batch of 10 engines. It seems scarcely credible that this immaculate piece of machinery was withdrawn from service just two and a half years later. After rusting away at Barry for many years, the engine was rescued by the British Railways Board and has now been lovingly restored as a sectioned exhibit at the National Railway Museum, York – a fitting end indeed./*G. H. Wheeler*

No 35001	Eastleigh	8/1959
No 35002	Eastleigh	5/1958
No 35003	Eastleigh	9/1959
No 35004	Eastleigh	7/1958
No 35005	Eastleigh	6/1959
No 35006	Eastleigh	10/1959
No 35007	Eastleigh	5/1958
No 35008	Eastleigh	5/1957
No 35009	Eastleigh	3/1957
No 35010	Eastleigh	1/1957
No 35011	Eastleigh	7/1959
No 35012	Eastleigh	2/1957
No 35013	Eastleigh	5/1956
No 35014	Eastleigh	7/1956

Left: Attached to No 35014 *Nederland Line*, at Nine Elms shed on 10 September 1966 is one of the 5250gal tenders which had new bodies on the existing frames, with externally a rather square appearance. Only one ladder was provided at the rear of these tenders, whereas the larger 6000gal tenders had two. The locomotive was withdrawn from service just six months later./*P. H. Groom*

Below left: No 35021 *New Zealand Line*, seen leaving Basingstoke, is attached to one of the modified 6000gal tenders and the longer wheelbase is very evident in this view, compared to the preceding illustration. Two ladders are provided at the rear, and the vacuum reservoirs are clearly seen under their protective

shield at the rear of the coal space. The removal of the side raves from the Bulleid Pacific tenders had the effect of eliminating pockets where surplus coal tended to accumulate uselessly, as well as facilitating the taking of water./*Alec Swain*

Below: A classic view of the 'Golden Arrow' Pullman, hauled by No 35015 *Rotterdam Lloyd*, in the truly immaculate condition in which Stewarts Lane kept the engines for this train. A small version of the arrow symbol (originally devised for the 'Britannia' Pacifics Nos 70004/14) adorns the smoke-deflectors, whilst the British and French flags catch the slipstream as the engine heads the train near Sydenham Hill, with steam visible from the whistle on the boiler side above the nameplate./*R. C. Riley*

No 35015	Eastleigh	6/1958
No 35016	Eastleigh	4/1957
No 35017	Eastleigh	3/1957
No 35018	Eastleigh	2/1956
No 35019	Eastleigh	5/1959
No 35020	Eastleigh	4/1956
No 35021	Eastleigh	6/1959
No 35022	Eastleigh	6/1956
No 35023	Eastleigh	2/1957
No 35024	Eastleigh	5/1959
No 35025	Eastleigh	12/1956
No 35026	Eastleigh	1/1957
No 35027	Eastleigh	5/1957
No 35028	Eastleigh	10/1959
No 35029	Eastleigh	9/1959
No 35030	Eastleigh	4/1958

It can be seen from the dates given above that authority to rebuild the remaining 15 locomotives quickly followed the initial order. In their rebuilt state the 'Merchant Navy' class proved more reliable than the original Bulleid creation, and they were still able to run at high speed when the opportunity presented itself.

Because the total withdrawal of steam traction was already well under way by the time the last engines had been rebuilt, they did not attain high mileages before withdrawals commenced in 1964, with only a few exceeding one million miles since building in their original Bulleid form.

First of Class Withdrawn: 35002/15 (1964)
Last of Class Withdrawn: 35003/7/8/13/23/30 (1967)
Examples Preserved: 35005/9*/28/9

**Not definitely preserved at time of writing.*

Top: Beautifully groomed for an enthusiast special no 35026 *Lamport and Holt Line* positively sparkles in this classic example of night photography, taken as the engine stands in the yard at Stockport Edgeley motive power depot. The balance weights added to the Bulleid-Firth-Brown driving wheels are particularly well illuminated, together with the clasp brake gear for the couplec wheels. The engine is attached to one of the rebodied 5250gal tenders./*J. R. Carter*

Above: No 35017 *Belgian Marine* standing in the carriage sidings at Clapham Junction. The imposing appearance of the rebuilt Bulleid Pacifics perhaps surpassed that of the BR standard engines which they resembled. In particular, the large-diameter chimney was very successfully shaped in the BR idiom, and the running plate (which was attached by brackets to the main frames, as opposed to the boiler) was at just the right height to give a balanced appearance to the engine, from whichever angle it was viewed. In this rear $\frac{3}{4}$ view the layout of the injectors, on the fireman's side, and the unusual location of the whistle on the boiler are particularly well illustrated./*Author*

Above: In the last years of steam on the Waterloo main line, Nine Elms motive power depot became a mecca for enthusiasts, many of them busy recording on film, tape and even canvas, the fast vanishing scene. A typical moment is depicted here, with shed staff pausing for discussion alongside No 35030 *Elder-Dempster Lines.* The speedometer drive on the rear coupled wheel is visible. */Eric Treacy*

Top: The final years of steam witnessed an abundance of rail tours, organised by the many enthusiast bodies. The rebuilt 'Merchant Navy' Pacifics had their share of the limelight in this exciting period, and certainly roamed further afield than would otherwise have been the case. Perhaps the most exciting rail route of all is the Settle and Carlisle stretch, with its powerful sense of machine versus the natural elements. In wet weather No 35012 *United States Lines* is seen working really hard as the train approaches the summit at Ais Gill. The train was the "Solway Ranger" railtour, organised by the Railway Correspondence & Travel Society. */John K. Morton*

Above: With nameplates and smokebox numberplate removed, No 35008 (formerly *Orient Line*) still makes a proud spectacle at Nine Elms on 3 May 1967 although withdrawn from service only two months later, when all the remaining Pacifics were made redundant. These were hectic days for the rail enthusiast – a final fling before the last steam worked main line services in Britain gave away to modernisation. The Pacifics themselves were far from life-expired, but no further use could be found for them. */J. Scrace.*

Right: No 35023 (formerly *Holland-Afrika Line*) had the dubious honour of powering the last steam working from Waterloo prior to complete electrification and dieselisation. This was the 8.30am Waterloo-Weymouth on 9 July 1967, seen here passing through Farnborough station. The engine was chosen because of a reputation it had gained for very fast running in the final days of steam. The same day as this photograph was taken, the remaining 'Merchant Navy' locomotives were withdrawn for scrap; these were Nos 35003/7/8/23/30.   Fate was kind to No 35028 *Clan Line*, which has been lovingly restored by enthusiasts, whilst No 35029 *Ellerman Lines* now survives in the National Railway Museum collection as a sectioned exhibit, having been rescued from Barry Scrapyard in 1973. Still in Barry, at the time of writing, was No 35009 *Shaw Savill*, whilst No 35005 *Canadian Pacific* was at Steamtown Carnforth, awaiting restoration./*G. P. Cooper*

4–6–2 Class 7P5F
Passenger Engines
(BR rebuild of Bulleid WC and BB class
Light Pacifics)
Introduced: 1957
Total: 60
Modified 'West Country' and 'Battle of Britain'

The first of the Light Pacifics to undergo modification was No 34005 *Barnstaple,* which appeared in the summer of 1957. The general effect was to produce a very similar locomotive to the modified 'Merchant Navy' class, and the technical changes are as detailed in the previous section (pages 78-89). One alteration was the widening of the cabs from 8ft 6in to 9ft for those locomotives which formerly had the

Below: The appearance of the rebuilt Light Pacifics closely followed that evolved for the 'Merchant Navy' class. One difference was the siting of the nameplates, which on the small engines were attached to a backplate bracketed to the running plate, whereas the 'Merchant Navy' nameplates were attached to the boiler sides. Rebuilt 'West Country' No 34017 *Ilfracombe* makes a fine study as she heads westward out of Salisbury with a Saturday extra, on 27 July 1963. Unlike their contemporary BR standard counterparts, the rebuilt Bulleid engines retained the electric lighting of the originals, a much-appreciated feature which was somewhat surprisingly not adopted by Riddles for his own Pacifics./*A. Richardson*

Top: A striking view of rebuilt 'West Country' Pacific No 34013 *Okehampton,* panned by the camera as the locomotive speeds through Drayton, near Chichester, with a Locomotive Club of Great Britain 'Isle of Wight Farewell Tour' special. The work of rebuilding the Light Pacifics began in 1957 (No 34005 *Barnstaple* was the first to appear from Eastleigh) and continued for four years, less a few days, by which time 60 engines had been dealt with./*David Hill*

Above: The rebuilt 'Battle of Britain' engines also had the position of the plaques and nameplates reversed, with the plaque now above the name in the same style as on the rebuilt 'West Country' Pacifics. No 34056 *Croydon* is particularly attractive in ex-works condition, at Eastleigh in October 1962./*G. Wheeler*

Above: The tender attached to No 34039 *Boscastle*, seen here at Eastleigh on 26 January 1959, has a new 5250gal body mounted on the original underframe. A few of these new bodies were built to replace badly corroded originals during the rebuilding scheme. Note BR power classification of 7P5FA on cabside above the number, with a yellow disc painted below to denote the use of the Bulleid TIA water treatment system. A yellow triangle painted in the same location was used to denote the use of BR water treatment./*C. P. Boocock*

Hastings gauge cab (see page 45) but other detail changes for the engines and for the tenders were as for the larger engines. One effect of the modification was to increase the engine weight to 90tons 1cwt in working order, compared to 86tons for the original design, which resulted in some route restrictions for the modified engines. In particular they were never allowed to Barnstaple, Ilfracombe or Padstow.

The rebuilding, which was initially authorised for 15 locomotives, extended to 60 examples before being brought to a halt. By this time (1961) the cost could no longer be justified and the remaining 50 engines worked out their lives in original form. No 34104 *Bere Alston* was the last to be modified in May 1961, and only lasted six years in this form before withdrawal.

The engines which were rebuilt were as follows:

Modified 'West Country' class

No 34001	Eastleigh	11/1957
No 34003	Eastleigh	9/1957
No 34004	Eastleigh	2/1958

No 34005	Eastleigh	6/1957
No 34008	Eastleigh	6/1960
No 34009	Eastleigh	1/1961
No 34010	Eastleigh	1/1959
No 34012	Eastleigh	1/1958
No 34013	Eastleigh	10/1957
No 34014	Eastleigh	3/1958
No 34016	Eastleigh	4/1958
No 34017	Eastleigh	11/1957
No 34018	Eastleigh	9/1958
No 34021	Eastleigh	12/1957
No 34022	Eastleigh	12/1957
No 34024	Eastleigh	2/1961
No 34025	Eastleigh	10/1957
No 34026	Eastleigh	2/1958
No 34027	Eastleigh	9/1957
No 34028	Eastleigh	8/1958
No 34029	Eastleigh	12/1958
No 34031	Eastleigh	11/1958
No 34032	Eastleigh	10/1960
No 34034	Eastleigh	8/1960
No 34036	Eastleigh	8/1960
No 34037	Eastleigh	3/1958
No 34039	Eastleigh	1/1959
No 34040	Eastleigh	10/1960

Above: With exhaust playing around the top of the smokebox. No 34090 *Sir Eustace Missenden, Southern Railway* races downhill towards Buckhorn Weston Tunnel, near Templecombe, with the 8.35 (SO) Waterloo to Exeter train on 7 September 1963. The engine retained its uniquely shaped nameplates upon rebuilding. A 4500gal tender was attached and the reduced width, to suit the Hastings line gauge, is very evident in this picture, compared to the engine and the leading carriage./*A. Richardson*

No 34042	Eastleigh	1/1959
No 34044	Eastleigh	5/1960
No 34045	Eastleigh	10/1958
No 34046	Eastleigh	2/1959
No 34047	Eastleigh	11/1958
No 34048	Eastleigh	3/1959
No 34093	Eastleigh	5/1960
No 34095	Eastleigh	1/1961
No 34096	Eastleigh	4/1961
No 34097	Eastleigh	2/1961
No 34098	Eastleigh	2/1961
No 34100	Eastleigh	9/1960
No 34101	Eastleigh	9/1960
No 34104	Eastleigh	5/1961
No 34108	Eastleigh	4/1961

Modified 'Battle of Britain' class

No 34050	Eastleigh	8/1958
No 34052	Eastleigh	9/1958
No 34053	Eastleigh	11/1958
No 34056	Eastleigh	12/1960
No 34058	Eastleigh	11/1960
No 34059	Eastleigh	3/1960
No 34060	Eastleigh	11/1960
No 34062	Eastleigh	3/1960
No 34071	Eastleigh	5/1960
No 34077	Eastleigh	7/1960
No 34082	Eastleigh	4/1960
No 34085	Eastleigh	6/1960
No 34087	Eastleigh	12/1960
No 34088	Eastleigh	4/1960
No 34089	Eastleigh	11/1960
No 34090	Eastleigh	8/1960
No 34109	Eastleigh	3/1961

As in the case of the modified 'Merchant Navy' class locomotives, the layout of the sanding gear was altered, partly because of the removal of the air-smoothed casing. The previous sand-

Left: With nameplates removed, but still retaining the large backplate, No 34004 (formerly *Yeovil*) heads the 8.46 am Bournemouth-Waterloo in Winchfield Cutting, as 'Merchant Navy' No 35030 (formerly *Elder-Dempster Lines*) approaches with the 10.24 am (SO) from Waterloo, on Saturday 10 June 1967, only weeks from the end of steam on the Southern./*G. P. Cooper*

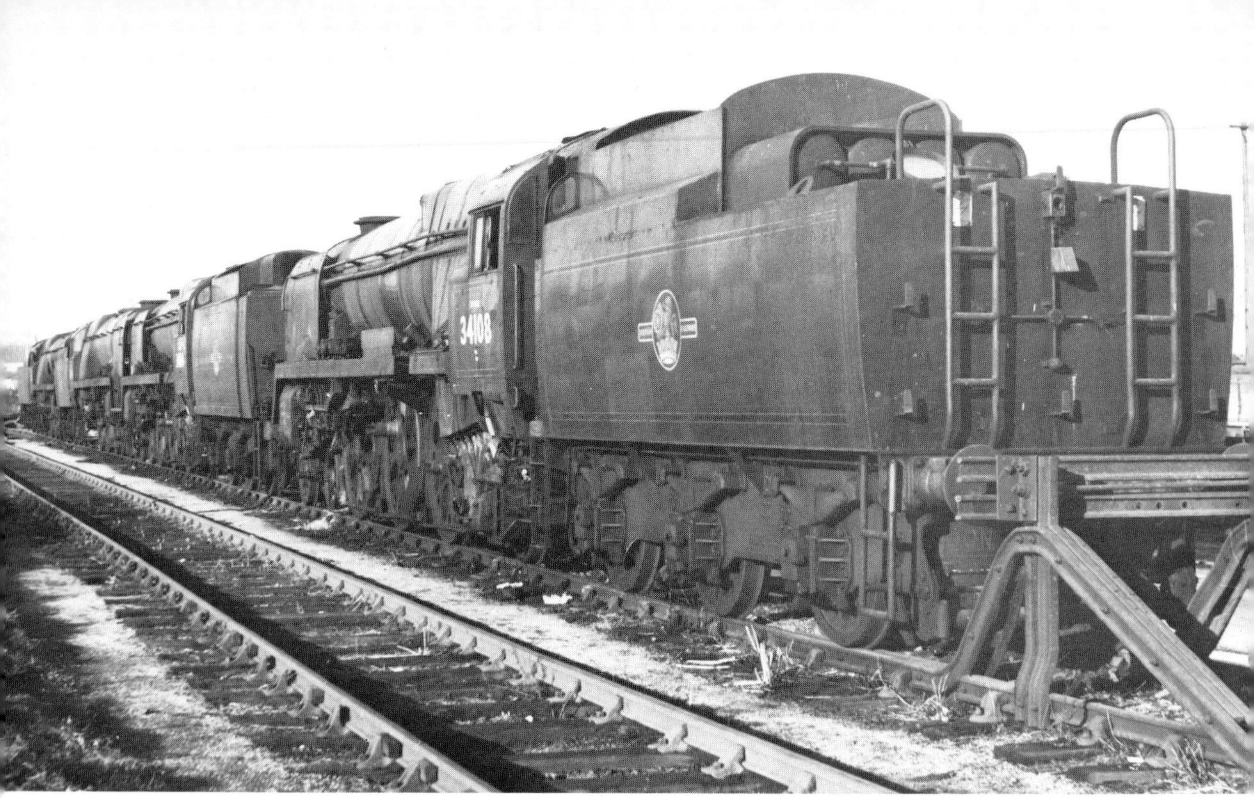
34108

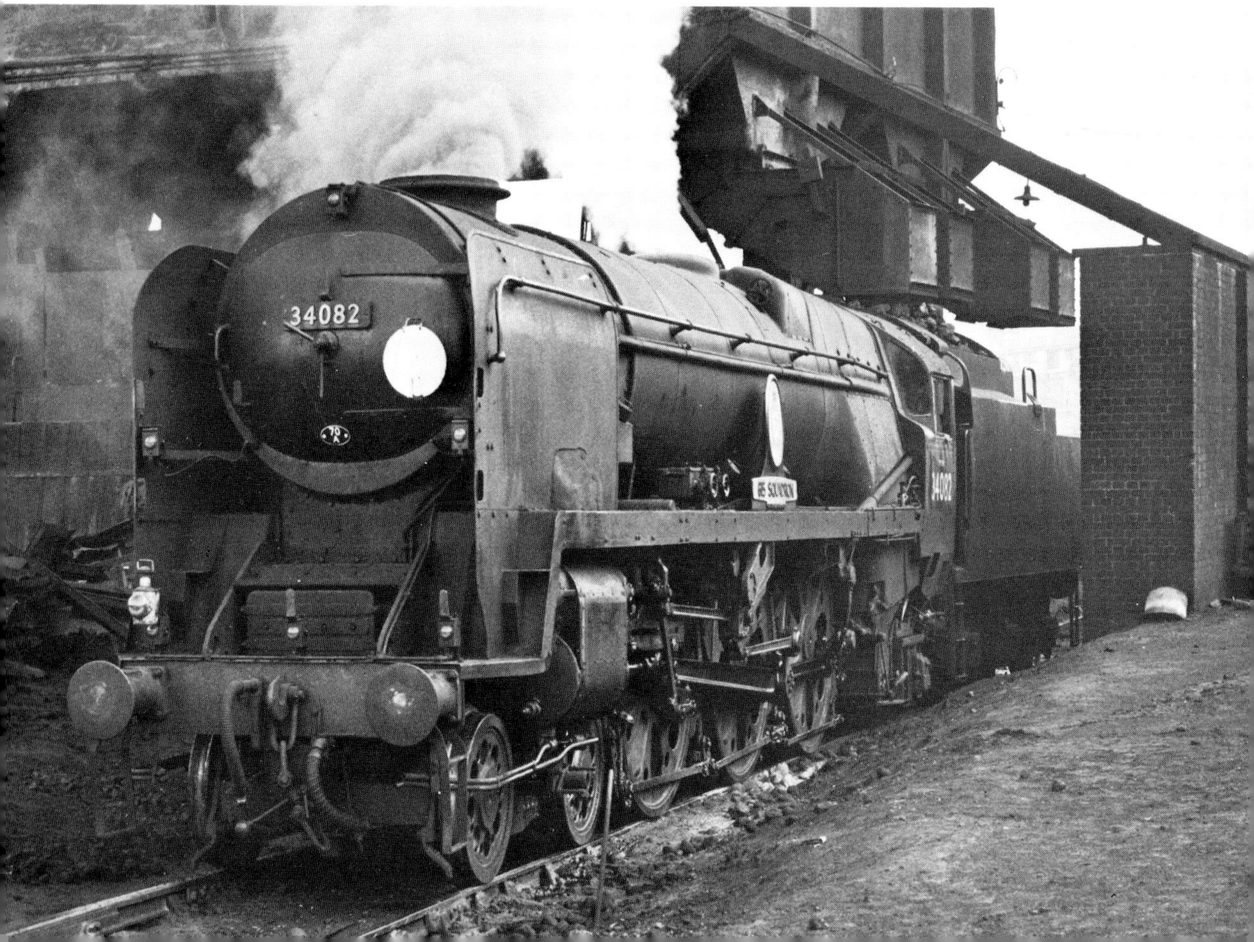
34082

Above left: Sad line-up of rebuilt Bulleid Light Pacifics at Newport, awaiting the cutting torch. Nearest the camera was No 34108 (formerly *Wincanton*) with Nos 34104 (ex *Bere Alston*) 34047 (ex *Callington*) and 34008 (ex *Padstow*,) in the background Photographed on 18 January 1968. The external condition of the engines emphasises their premature withdrawal, with many years of useful life still left in them./*N. E. Preedy*

Left: Rebuilt Light Pacific No 34082 *615 Squadron* under the coaling-plant at Nine Elms MPD. The battery box for the BR AWS system is clearly visible on the front footplate below the smokebox./*Eric Treacy*

Above: No 34001 (formerly *Exeter*), the pioneer 'West Country' Pacific in final rebuilt form, is seen banking an up relief boat train at Upwey Wishing Well Halt on 30 June 1967 – just a few days before withdrawal./*Derek Cross*

boxes were replaced by new ones; those for the leading pair of wheels were placed above the footplate adjacent to the back of the smokebox, and those for the driving pair of wheels were between the frames, fed by fillers above the footplate. Steam sanding gear, applied to the leading and driving wheels, was arranged for forward running, but in addition steam sandpipes were provided behind the driving wheels for reverse running; these replaced the gravity sanding gear, which was previously fitted to the front end of the tender for this purpose.

It was rebuild No 34089 *602 Squadron* which had the dubious honour of being the last steam locomotive to be repaired at Eastleigh, leaving the works on 3 October 1966 and remaining in traffic for only another eight months or so, before the final withdrawals took place.

First of (Modified) Class Withdrawn: 34028 (1964)
Last of (Modified) Class Withdrawn: 34001/4/13/18/21/24/25/36/37/52/60/87/89/90/93/95. (1967).
Examples Preserved: 34016/39.
(At the time of writing it was possible that Nos 34028/58, 34101 would be preserved)

Appendix 1

Electric Locomotives

The Electrical Engineer of the Southern Railway for almost the entire period that O. V. S. Bulleid was the Chief Mechanical Engineer, was Alfred Raworth. Bulleid and Raworth held opposing views on some aspects of the SR electrification programme, but nevertheless they collaborated most successfully on the design and production of three large electric locomotives. Bulleid was responsible for their mechanical portions and their maintenance in service. The external appearance of these locomotives was also influenced by Bulleid's views on aesthetics and function and had the same somewhat austere finish which characterised his multiple-unit electric stock in the 1940/50 period.

Below: Devoid of lettering or numerals, except for the Bulleid numbering CCI on the bufferbeams, and finished in grey livery with white stripes, the first electric locomotive emerged from Ashford Works in 1941, and is seen here posed for the official photographer at Lover's Walk, Brighton soon after completion. The box-like body and massive underframe certainly gave a solid look to the locomotive, which was mounted on two six-wheel bogies of Bulleid design with BFB (Bulleid-Firth-Brown) wheels of 3ft 6in diameter. The locomotive weighed 99tons and was 56ft 9in long overall; tractive effort was 40 000lb./*British Rail SR*

Bottom: Intended as a mixed-traffic type, the electric locomotive had to be capable of bridging the gaps in the conductor rail which existed at various points on the system. This was, of course, a necessity when operating loose-coupled goods trains, or when starting away from a station. The solution was found in a novel way, by providing a "booster" unit in the form of a flywheel-driven generator which enabled some power to continue to be supplied to the locomotive whilst traversing the short gaps. No CCI is seen here with a southbound goods working at Merstham on 5 December 1941. Somewhat surprising was the lack of electric headlights, although a headcode panel was provided./*British Rail SR*

Top: A second basically similar locomotive, No CC2, emerged from Ashford Works in 1943 with some improvements based on experience in traffic with the prototype. The provision of combined electric headlamps and marker discs and multiple-unit jumper cables made the front ends more businesslike in appearance. No CC2, seen here in post-war Malachite green livery, also displays the pantograph which was fitted to all three locomotives, to enable them to operate in goods yards where there was no third rail. Special tramway-type catenary was designed for such locations. The headcode panel, which was a feature of No CC1, was not fitted to CC2./*British Rail SR*

Above: The third of the Bulleid/Raworth Co-Co electric locomotives was a more powerful machine with a tractive effort of 45 000lb and increased length and weight of 58ft 3in and 105 tons respectively. The appearance was even more box-like, with a blunt front end style similar to that of the post war Bulleid electric suburban multiple-units. No 20003 did not appear until after nationalisation, in October 1948, and was finished in Malachite green with Gill Sans numerals and lettering, with yellow lining. When this official photograph was taken, at Lovers Walk Brighton, the roof pantograph had not yet been fitted (see photograph at bottom of page 100)./*British Rail SR*

Below: In the black and aluminium BR livery, No 20001 is seen entering Streatham with a 12coach special of LMR stock, conveying delegates to the International Union of Railways Congress on an excursion from Eastbourne to Bath. Comparison with the pictures on page 98-99 shows some alteration to the front end, with headlights and marker discs added and the route indicator panel blanked-off, also repositioned vacuum pipe and hose./*R. C. Riley*

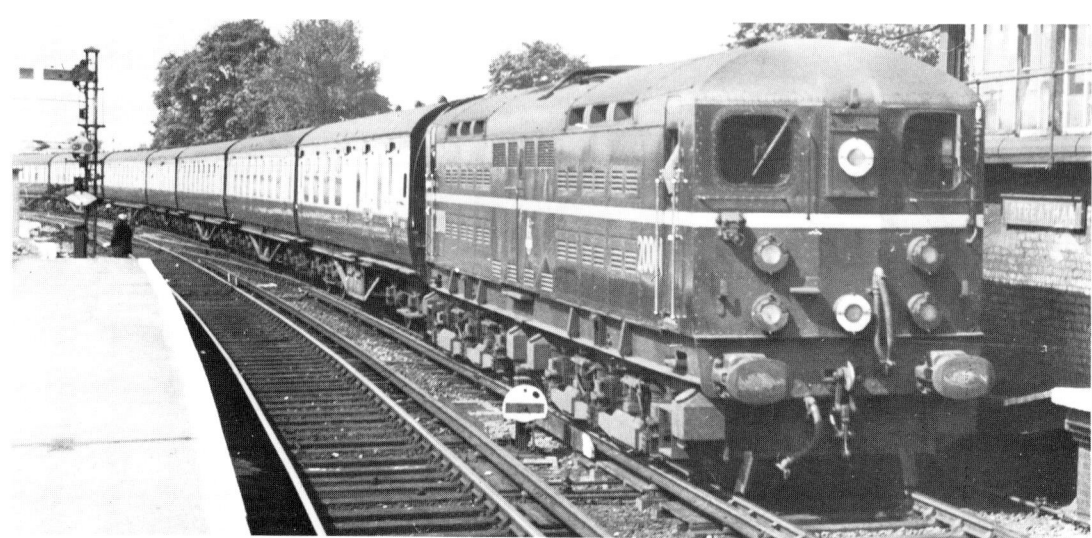

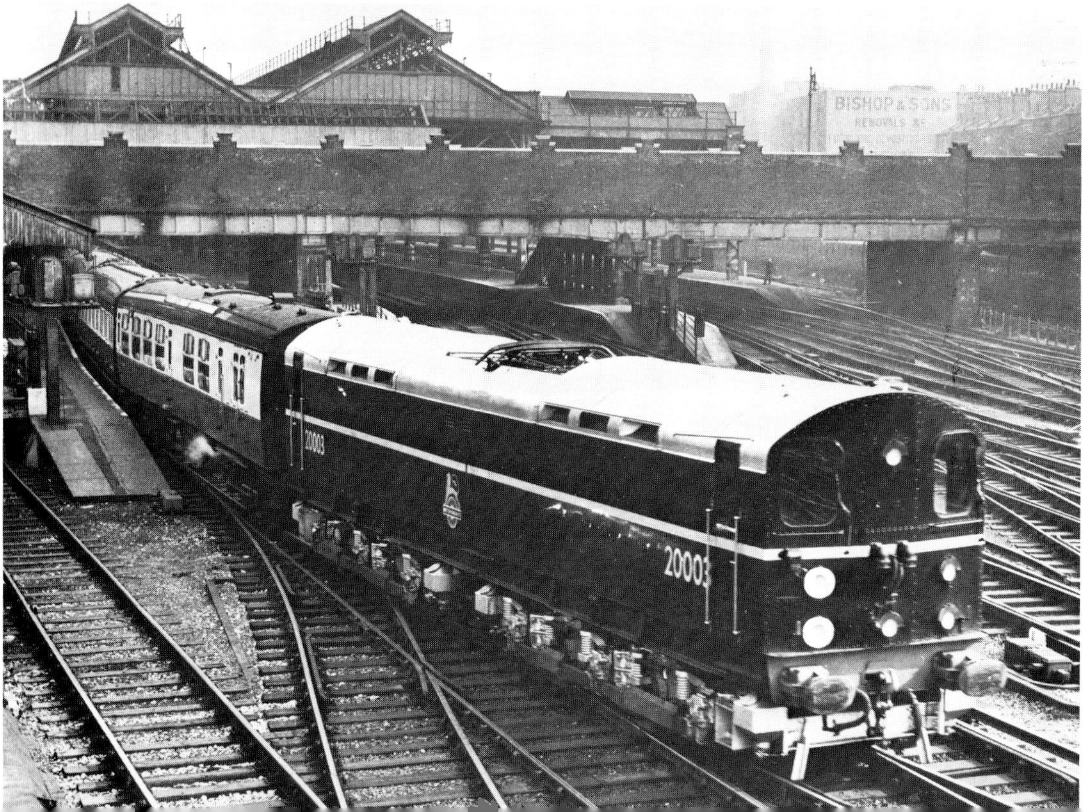

Bottom left: The early BR livery of black with aluminium roof, bogies and lining, applied circa 1949/50, certainly altered the appearance of Nos CC1/2 (which were renumbered 20001/2) and No 20003, which latter presents a bold face at the head of the Newhaven boat train (in red and cream livery) leaving Victoria on 6 April 1950. The roof well with the pantograph is clearly visible. */British Rail SR*

Below: An attractive livery of BR locomotive green with red and white lining and pale grey-green frames was applied in the late 1950s, as seen on No 20002, photographed at Eastleigh on 21 July 1959. This locomotive carried an experimental light blue livery for a period in 1948/9, as part of a proposed new BR scheme, and was exhibited to the Railway Executive at Kensington Addison Road Station./*L. Elsey*

Above: The final livery scheme of BR rail blue, with yellow warning on the front ends and twin air horns on the cab roof. The route indicator headcode panel had been restored to use (and the headlamps removed) on No 20001 in its last years of service, seen here as the locomotive heads a Derby Day Royal Train to Tattenham Corner from Victoria and passes Reedham on 31 May 1968. Despite the immaculate appearance of the locomotive, its days were numbered and, together with No 20002, it was withdrawn in the following December. The last of the trio to be built, No 20003, in fact was the first to go, in October 1968. They were popular and efficient locomotives./*J. Scrace*

Appendix 2

Diesel Locomotives

A brief pictorial review is presented of the diesel locomotive designs which appeared whilst O. V. S. Bulleid was Chief Mechanical Engineer, both in Britain and Eire. His actual involvement in their design varied considerably, although the mechanical portions were under his control and were somewhat influenced by his views on locomotive appearance, as in the case of the SR electrics. In retrospect it is clear that whilst on the SR Bulleid was not over-enthusiastic where diesel power was concerned, but his enthusiasm grew for the massive CIE dieselisation programme in later years. His three SR main line locomotives were nevertheless to have an appreciable influence on the form of the Pilot Scheme diesels of comparable power produced by British Railways.

Right: Towards the end of 1946 the Southern Railway decided to build three ICo-Col diesel-electric locomotives for express passenger service, and by July 1947 the design of these was under way. Not until 1951, however, did the first unit, No 10201, appear from Ashford Works, well after the retirement of O.V.S. Bulleid. This locomotive, and the second one, had 1750 hp English Electric 16-cylinder diesel engines similar to the 1600hp version installed in the pioneer LMS mixed-traffic Nos 10000/1. (It is worth placing on record that Nos 10201-3 were in fact first considered before the LMS design, but were delayed in authorisation.) Six nose-suspended, axle-hung traction motors were provided driving three axles on each bogie. The design of the bogie closely followed that used for the three electric locomotives (see pages 98-101), but had an additional axle, for weight carrying purposes, in the form of a pony truck. Maximum tractive effort was 31 200lb and the weight in working order was 135tons. The fuel oil capacity was 1150gal. Overall length of the locomotives was 63ft 9in. The black and silver livery at first applied was similar to that introduced by the LMS for their diesel-electric Co-Cos./*British Rail SR*

Above: Clear Bulleid influence is apparent in the Boxpok wheels of 500 hp diesel-mechanical No 11001. This shunting engine was designed by the Southern but did not appear until after nationalisation, in 1950. It was constructed at Ashford and was powered by a 12-cylinder V-type Paxman engine with a three-speed gearbox. It weighed 49½tons in full working order and was 33ft 3in over buffers. Intended for heavy shunting and short-distance transfer and trip work, No 11001 was transferred to the Leeds area for some time, later returning to the SR which withdrew it after a life of only nine years, in August 1959./*Ian Allan Library*

Above: The third of the Bulleid main-line diesel-electrics was rated at 2000hp and was in some ways the precursor of the Pilot scheme BR Type 4 designs. It was three tons lighter, at 132tons, than Nos 10201/2. The original black and silver livery was later replaced by BR standard locomotive green with orange and black lining and, for some odd reason, a primrose yellow roof, which soon dirtied down. No 10203 was photographed in service on the LMR main line near Tring with a freight, on 24 March 1959. Bulleid shaped the exterior of these diesels to match the profile of his own post-war carriages, and he intended that they should be finished in a matching Malachite green livery. /*G. J. Jefferson*

Above: With air horns perched on the roof in place of the original chime whistle, Nos 10203 and 10201 stand forlorn at Derby in their final state, with yellow warning panels above the bufferbeam. Condemned to a comparatively early withdrawal the Bulleid design nevertheless influenced the first generation BR diesel-electrics, in particular the bogie design which was applied to both the BR Sulzer Peak and the English Electric Type 4. */Ian Allan Library*

Left: For a period in 1954 the Southern tried out No 10202 on the 'Golden Arrow' and 'Night Ferry' services, the same engine working all four trains each day. The engine is seen here leaving Victoria with the 1.00pm 'Golden Arrow' service to Folkestone – in no way so colourful as the normal Pacific! */British Rail SR*

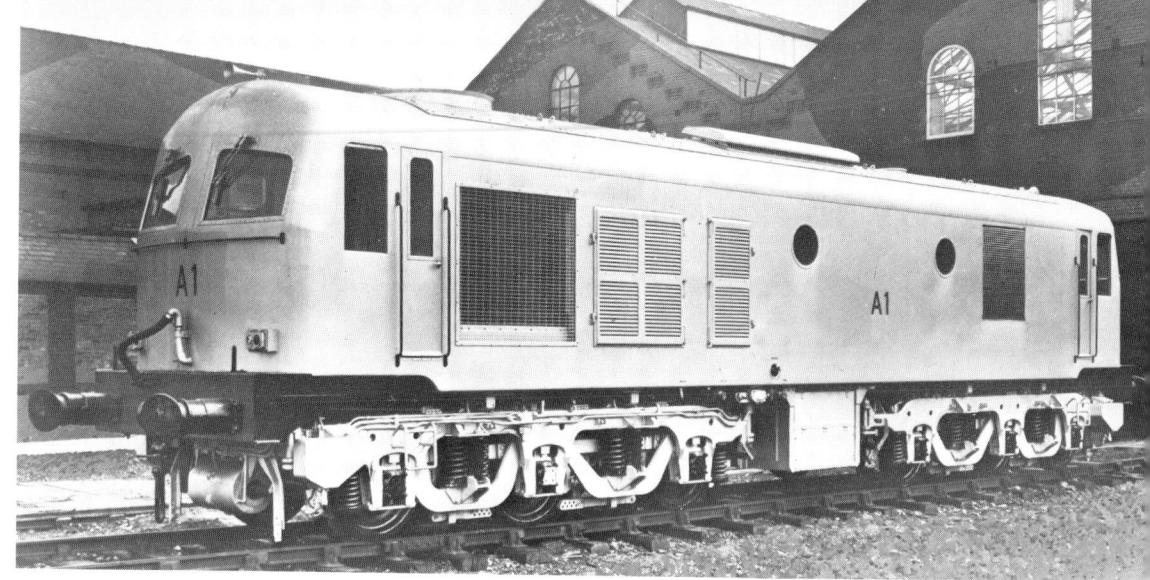

Above: Although Bulleid fought for residual use of turf-burning steam locomotives for peak and emergency traffic in the shape of his 'Turf Burner' No CC1 (see page 74), he masterminded the CIE switch to dieselisation for future locomotive construction, and drew up a plan for total conversion. In 1953 tenders were invited from many builders in other countries. The orders were placed with Metropolitan-Vickers for 60 1 200 hp diesel-electric Co-Cos and 34 smaller Bo-Bos (see bottom left). The 1 200 hp design was designated class A and appeared in 1955. They were fabricated by Metro-Cammell in Birmingham and erected in the former LNER carriage shops at Dukinfield, Manchester, with Crossley engines./ *Ian Allan Library*

Centre left: Delivery of the class A diesel-electrics was completed by January 1957. By the time No A34 was photographed, in August 1959, the original livery had been replaced by a bright green which suited them better. They were not wholly efficient locomotives in their original form and recent years have seen extensive modifications, including fitting entirely new engines of General Motors design. No A34 was photographed leaving Dundalk with a Dublin bound goods./ *Frank Church*

Bottom left: CIE Class C diesel electric No C202 stands at Drimoleague (Cork, Bandon and South Coast section) with the 2.20 pm from Baltimore, consisting of veteran six-wheelers, on 15 July 1957. The class was designed for secondary and branch line work and had a Bo-Bo wheel arrangement. An order was placed for 34 of these Crossley-engined 550hp locomotives, which were finished in an unexciting metallic silver-grey livery. Chief influence on the appearance was the builder, Metropolitan-Vickers, although Bulleid kept a close watch on design progress, as in the case of the larger class A and B designs./ *C. P. Boocock*

Top: Some time before Bulleid arrived in Ireland the CIE had ordered ten Sulzer 950 hp diesel engines. These engines, used in pairs, were intended to power five main-line diesel locomotives of 1900hp. The engines had actually arrived in packing cases at Dublin Docks when the locomotives were cancelled. For some years they lay idle before being utilised in ten Class B AIA-AIA diesels of 950hp, with bodywork by the Birmingham Railway Carriage & Wagon Co.; numbered B101-112. In service they proved more reliable than the A and C class diesels with Crossley engines. Their appearance differed somewhat from the other two classes because of the use of three cab windows of neater proportions./*Ian Allan Library*

Above: For shunting duties the CIE ordered 19 small diesel-hydraulics, with Maybach engines and Mekydro transmissions, of German origin. Bulleid decided that the CIE could construct the mechanical portions at Inchicore, where assembly of the locomotives took place. These were numbered E 401-419 and were completed in 1954. A further 14 locomotives were built at Inchicore in 1961. No E404 is seen approaching Amiens Street, Dublin with a goods on 1 August 1959./*Frank Church*

Appendix 3

Named Locomotives

This list shows all named Bulleid locomotives, with their original numbers and later BR numbers. Locomotives delivered after nationalisation (1948 onwards) are shown in italics.

The original Bulleid numbering scheme was highly unusual and was an adaptation of Continental practice, based on the number of axles on a locomotive, not the wheels. Thus a 4-6-2 was a 21C. The '2' represented two leading carrying axles, i.e. the bogie; the '1' represented one trailing carrying axle, i.e. the truck; and the C represented the three coupled axles (based on A as 1, B as 2, C as 3 etc.) Added to this was the number of each individual locomotive, 21C1 being No 1 of the class, and so on.

Bulleid's nameplates were a particularly attractive feature of his engines, in many cases having a pictorial motif in addition to the lettering, which added colour to their appearance.

In the following lists, locomotives marked with an asterisk (*) are those rebuilt by British Railways.

4-6-2 Class MN BR class 8P
'Merchant Navy' (see page 18 and 78*)

*21C1 *(35001)* Channel Packet
*21C2 *(35002)* Union Castle
*21C3 *(35003)* Royal Mail
*21C4 *(35004)* Cunard White Star
*21C5 *(35005)* Canadian Pacific
*21C6 *(35006)* Peninsular & Oriental S.N. Co.
*21C7 *(35007)* Aberdeen Commonwealth
*21C8 *(35008)* Orient Line
*21C9 *(35009)* Shaw Savill
*21C10 *(35010)* Blue Star
*21C11 *(35011)* General Steam Navigation
*21C12 *(35012)* United States Lines
*21C13 *(35013)* Blue Funnel (1)
*21C14 *(35014)* Nederland Line
*21C15 *(35015)* Rotterdam Lloyd
*21C16 *(35016)* Elders Fyffes
*21C17 *(35017)* Belgian Marine
*21C18 *(35018)* British India Line
*21C19 *(35019)* French Line C.G.T.
*21C20 *(35020)* Bibby Line
35021 New Zealand Line
35022 Holland-America Line
35023 Holland-Afrika Line
35024 East Asiatic Company

35025 Brocklebank Line
35026 Lamport & Holt Line
35027 Port Line
35028 Clan Line
35029 Ellerman Lines
35030 Elder-Dempster Lines

(1) At first named Blue Funnel Line, later became Blue Funnel Certum Pete Finem

4-6-2 Class WC BR class 7P5F 'West Country' (see pages 44 and 90*)

*21C101 *(34001)* Exeter
 21C102 *(34002)* Salisbury
*21C103 *(34003)* Plymouth
*21C104 *(34004)* Yeovil
*21C105 *(34005)* Barnstaple
 21C106 *(34006)* Bude
 21C107 *(34007)* Wadebridge
*21C108 *(34008)* Padstow
*21C109 *(34009)* Lyme Regis
*21C110 *(34010)* Sidmouth
 21C111 *(34011)* Tavistock
*21C112 *(34012)* Launceston
*21C113 *(34013)* Okehampton
*21C114 *(34014)* Budleigh Salterton
 21C115 *(34015)* Exmouth
*21C116 *(34016)* Bodmin
*21C117 *(34017)* Ilfracombe
*21C118 *(34018)* Axminster
 21C119 *(34019)* Bideford
 21C120 *(34020)* Seaton
*21C121 *(34021)* Dartmoor
*21C122 *(34022)* Exmoor
 21C123 *(34023)* Blackmore Vale (2)
*21C124 *(34024)* Tamar Valley
*21C125 *(34025)* Whimple (3)
*21C126 *(34026)* Yes Tor
*21C127 *(34027)* Taw Valley
*21C128 *(34028)* Eddystone
*21C129 *(34029)* Lundy
 21C130 *(34030)* Watersmeet
*21C131 *(34031)* Torrington
*21C132 *(34032)* Camelford
 21C133 *(34033)* Chard
*21C134 *(34034)* Honiton
 21C135 *(34035)* Shaftesbury
*21C136 *(34036)* Westward Ho
*21C137 *(34037)* Clovelly
 21C138 *(34038)* Lynton
*21C139 *(34039)* Boscastle
*21C140 *(34040)* Crewkerne
 21C141 *(34041)* Wilton
*21C142 *(34042)* Dorchester
 21C143 *(34043)* Combe Martin

*21C144 *(34044)* Woolacombe
*21C145 *(34045)* Ottery St. Mary
*21C146 *(34046)* Braunton
*21C147 *(34047)* Callington
*21C148 *(34048)* Crediton

 34091 *Weymouth*
 34092 *City of Wells (4)*
*34093 *Saunton*
 34094 *Mortehoe*
*34095 *Brentor*
*34096 *Trevone*
*34097 *Holsworthy*
*34098 *Templecombe*
 34099 *Lynmouth*
*34100 *Appledore*
*34101 *Hartland*
 34102 *Lapford*
 34103 *Calstock*
*34104 *Bere Alston*
 34105 *Swanage*
 34106 *Lydford*
 34107 *Blandford Forum (5)*
*34108 *Wincanton*

(2) At first named 'Blackmoor Vale'; altered in 1950
(3) No 21C125 'Whimple' was at first named 'Rough Tor' (for a few days only).
(4) Named 'Wells' until November 1949.
(5) Named 'Blandford' until October 1952.

4-6-2 Class BB BR class 7P5F 'Battle of Britain' (see pages 56 and 90*)

 21C149 *(34049)* Anti-Aircraft Command
*21C150 *(34050)* Royal Observer Corps

Above left: Left hand nameplate of 'Merchant Navy' Pacific No 21C3 (35003) *Royal Mail*, in original state with the engine finished in matt Malachite green, with yellow lining./*Author's collection*

Left: 'Battle of Britain' class No 34084 *253 Squadron*, in unmodified form, with BR dark green livery and orange and black lining. Sandbox fillers located each side of the decorative oval enamel plaque./*D. H. Cape*

Above: Right hand nameplate of 'West Country' class Pacific No 34003, after conversion, with the plates supported by a backplate (see page 94.) In the unmodified form, the decorative plaque was located below the nameplate./*Author's collection*

Right: Waiting in the queue to be coaled at Nine Elms shed, on 15 March 1958, rebuilt 'Merchant Navy' No 35010 *Blue Star* receives some oil. Balance weight on centre driving wheel clearly visible./*Derek Harman*

21C151 *(34051)* Winston Churchill
*21C152 *(34052)* Lord Dowding
*21C153 *(34053)* Sir Keith Park
21C154 *(34054)* Lord Beaverbrook
21C155 *(34055)* Fighter Pilot
*21C156 *(34056)* Croydon
21C157 *(34057)* Biggin Hill
*21C158 *(34058)* Sir Frederick Pile
*21C159 *(34059)* Sir Archibald Sinclair
*21C160 *(34060)* 25 Squadron
21C161 *(34061)* 73 Squadron
*21C162 *(34062)* 17 Squadron
21C163 *(34063)* 229 Squadron
21C164 *(34064)* Fighter Command
21C165 *(34065)* Hurricane
21C166 *(34066)* Spitfire
21C167 *(34067)* Tangmere
21C168 *(34068)* Kenley
21C169 *(34069)* Hawkinge
21C170 *(34070)* Manston
*34071 *601 Squadron* (6)
*34072 *257 Squadron*
*34073 *249 Squadron*
*34074 *46 Squadron*
*34075 *264 Squadron*
*34076 *41 Squadron*
*34077 *603 Squadron*
*34078 *222 Squadron*
*34079 *141 Squadron*
*34080 *74 Squadron*
*34081 *92 Squadron*
*34082 *615 Squadron*
*34083 *605 Squadron*
*34084 *253 Squadron*
*34085 *501 Squadron*
*34086 *219 Squadron*
*34087 *145 Squadron*
*34088 *213 Squadron*
*34089 *602 Squadron*
*34090 *Sir Eustace Missenden, Southern Railway*
*34109 *Sir Trafford Leigh-Mallory*
*34110 *66 Squadron*

(6) Carried the name '615 Squadron' for a short period in 1948.

The 'Leader' class 0–6–6–0T design (see page 66) was intended to carry names, but did not survive long enough for such adornment. The original Bulleid notation would have been Nos CC101-105 and names known to have been selected by Bulleid himself for the first two were *Missenden* and *Churchill,* although these were actually carried by 'Battle of Britain' class engines in slightly different form.

Bibliography

Reference was made to the following books and periodicals whilst compiling this Pictorial History. The reader seeking further information on O. V. S. Bulleid, his life and his locomotives, is recommended to them:

Bulleid, H. A. V. *Master Builders of Steam.* Ian Allan Ltd.
Day-Lewis, S. *Bulleid – Last Giant of Steam.* George Allen & Unwin.
Nock, O. S. *Southern Steam.* David & Charles.
Allen, Cecil J. and Townroe, S.C. *Bulleid Pacifics of the Southern Railway.* Ian Allan Ltd.
Reed, Brian *Merchant Navy Pacifics Loco-Profile No. 22* Profile Publications
Rowledge, J. W. P. *The Turf Burner. Ireland's last steam locomotive design.* Irish Railway Record Society.
Winkworth, D. W. *Bulleid's Pacifics* George Allen & Unwin.

Various issues of the following periodicals and journals:

The Locomotive
Trains Illustrated/Modern Railways.
Railway Gazette
Railway Magazine
Railway World
Railway Observer (RCTS)
SLS Journal

Below: The most striking of the named train adornments were those produced for the 'Golden Arrow' service, with British and French flags on the front and a huge arrow along the side. The engines were always specially smart and made a pleasing spectacle, as evidenced by No 34086 *219 Squadron*, seen here in full cry on a wintry day in the Kent countryside. The engine has AWS equipment on the front, and a rebuilt tender. */Derek Cross*